D0338458

Adult Survivors of Childhood Emotional, Physical, and Sexual Abuse: Dynamics and Treatment

by Francisco Gaspar Cruz, M.D.
and Laura Essen, L.C.S.W.

JASON ARONSON INC.
Northvale, New Jersey
London

This book was set in 11-point Goudy by Lind Graphics of Upper Saddle River, New Jersey, and printed and bound by Haddon Craftsmen of Scranton, Pennsylvania.

Copyright © 1994 by Jason Aronson Inc.

10 9 8 7 6 5 4 3 2 1

Library of Congress Cataloging-in-Publication Data

Cruz, Francisco Gaspar.
    Adult survivors of childhood emotional, physical, and sexual abuse :
    dynamics and treatment / by Francisco Gaspar Cruz and Laura Essen.
      p. cm.
    Includes bibliographical references and index.
    ISBN 0-87668-406-1
    1. Adult child abuse victims. I. Essen, Laura. II. Title.
    [DNLM: 1. Child Abuse—psychology. 2. Child of Impaired Parents—
    psychology. 3. Psychotherapy—methods. WM 420 C957a 1994]
    RC569.5.C55C78 1994
    616.85'8369—dc20
    DNLM/DLC
    for Library of Congress   93-30599

Manufactured in the United States of America. Jason Aronson Inc. offers books and cassettes. For information and catalog write to Jason Aronson Inc., 230 Livingston Street, Northvale, New Jersey 07647.

To the memory of Francisco E. Cruz, M.D.,
who inspired me to always keep hope
and find the light in the midst of human pain.
—Francisco G. Cruz, M.D.

To all victims of childhood abuse who did not survive
and to those who continue to suffer its aftermath.

To my patients, past and present,
who continually contribute to my profound sense of awe
at the human spirit
and the struggle for meaningful psychological growth.
—Laura Essen, L.C.S.W.

Contents

Preface

This book was conceived in the context of a collegial clinical relationship between the authors. In working with patients who shared many similar clinical situations, we were able to see different clinical dimensions of our patients in their weekly professional interchanges. Because of our different clinical backgrounds and training we became acutely aware of the need to make use of complementary theories to do comprehensive clinical work with patients with past traumatic experience. We realized that an eclectic clinical approach was conducive to more effective work with this patient population. Keeping in mind different development models and part-theories helped us maintain an integrated view of the patient's developmental vicissitudes vis-à-vis the impact the childhood trauma may have had in those different developmental currents, such as structural development, separation-individuation processes, cognition, object relations, self-development and integration.

The mixed clinical presentations necessarily require an eclectic technique based on whatever deficits or conflicts are identified in the diagnostic and evaluation process and in the context of the patient's developmental vicissitudes. This book is an attempt to integrate seemingly divergent or contradictory clinical views into more coherent and comprehensive ways of formulating clinical intervention when working with adult survivors of childhood physical, emotional, or sexual abuse.

We are grateful to our teachers, clinical supervisors, and colleagues who contributed to our professional development and whose diverging clinical points of view influenced the attempt at clinical integration reflected in this book. We would also like to express our appreciation to Dr. Jason Aronson for his enthusiasm and confidence in this project, together with a special thank you to Cindy Sterling, our literary agent, for her unfailing support. We would like to thank the editorial staff at Jason Aronson Publishers, especially Judith Cohen, our production editor, and Giselle Weiss, our copy editor, whose valuable editing and suggestions gave final form to our book. We hope this book will make a contribution to the treatment of adult survivors of childhood traumatic disorders.

Acknowledgments

I would like to acknowledge all my colleagues and friends at the Menninger Clinic where I received my training and experience. To Amado Muñiz, M.D., who guided me in my first steps in the psychiatric field, to Jack Ross, Becquer Benalcazar, Leonard Horowitz, Sam Bradshaw, Alfred Namnum, Stuart Averil, Jerome Katz, Irwin Rosen, among others, for their enlightening training, their supervision, and friendship; to Maggie Dajer, who typed my first manuscript; to my students and supervisees with appreciation for challenging and stimulating my clinical thinking; to my mother, who always encouraged me not to give up on my life goals even in the worst moments; to my wife and children for their patience and tolerance for my taking time away from them to complete this project.

Francisco Gaspar Cruz, M.D.

A book is not only created by those who directly write it but, additionally, by those kind people who so generously give of themselves to the author along the way, even before the conception of the dream or its realization. Therefore, I am truly grateful to those people who have touched my life along the journey to the completion of this book. While it is impossible to acknowledge the contributions of all who helped bring this book to fruition, I want to especially note my gratitude and appreciation to the following people:

The outstanding professors at the Florida International University and Barry University schools of social work for my earliest professional training and development, who contributed to a thirst for knowledge that has not yet been quenched.

My three clinical supervisors: Robin Stilwell, M.S., who greatly assisted and acknowledged me during the early years of my clinical training—her support has been invaluable to me; Sherri Siegel, L.C.S.W., whose training, encouragement, and unfailing support has been so helpful to me throughout my career; Yael Heimer, L.C.S.W., from whom I have learned a great deal because of her unique and remarkable training approach and whose close friendship has proved enriching to me over the years.

Professor Celia Zayas-Bazan, L.C.S.W., of Barry University, who demonstrated to her students the art of helping people, for which I am very grateful.

Marian Sneider, L.C.S.W., to whom I would like to express my deepest heartfelt gratitude for believing in me long before I believed in myself, for serving as my role model as a clinical social worker, and for giving so generously of herself. Her profound effect and influence is with me always.

Ray Armstrong, Ph.D., who took the time to read and critique Chapter 3 of the book and whose initial support was so meaningful.

Ursula Sunshine Assaid, subject of *Death from Child Abuse . . . And No One Heard*, by Dana Weikel and Eve Krupinski, who has touched the recesses of my soul in such a way that I will never quite be the same. Like the authors of that book, I, too, am sorry that I was not there for you. Hopefully, this book will create enough of a therapeutic change that the suffering victims endure will greatly diminish. I would also like to thank the authors for their more than generous contribution to the mental health field in general and to this book in particular.

Dora Posada, L.C.S.W., whose positive support and encouragement during the many years of our friendship is gratefully appreciated. Cornellia Philipson, for her enthusiasm, support, friendship and belief in this project. Anne Levine, for whose love and special friendship I am truly thankful. Liz Taylor, for being there for me with her expertise when I needed her. I am so grateful.

Rita and Martin Ammerman, my parents, who loved and nourished my heart and soul during the most significant years of my life and whose endless support and confidence during this entire process will always be deeply treasured.

Rose Swartz, my grandmother, whose unconditional love is forever with me; I am truly sorry she is not here to share this book with me.

Elena Essen Endara and Michael Essen, who taught me how profoundly precious and magical children are. My heartfelt gratitude for your love, understanding, and tolerance, which allowed me to "sing a better song."

Richard Essen, my loving husband, who dispels the myth that one person cannot make a difference, because he most certainly has made such a remarkable difference in this book. I am forever grateful for his contributions. His initial support and belief in this project from its birth and his never ending dedication, love, and work with this project have enriched its quality.

Those patients of mine who shared their plight so selflessly in order to ease the pain of others. You have my deepest respect and appreciation.

Christopher Endara, my son-in-law, who worked enthusiastically on the art project in Chapter 4 and for whose caring and interest I am very grateful.

Patricia Minnich, who came to the rescue by doing an outstanding job of typing the entire manuscript—my deepest appreciation.

My many friends and acquaintances in Miami Lakes, Florida, and in particular Betty Bender, Lee Grayson, Eve Rozgonyi, and Jack McCall, who have been a seemingly endless source of warmth, interest, and encouragement. You have my sincerest thanks.

Barry Berger, a natural healer. Wherever you are, thank you so much for being there for me at the right time, in the right way, in the right place. My gratitude forever.

Laura Essen, L.C.S.W.

Introduction

The incidence of child abuse is all too common. Included are sexual, physical, and emotional abuse and neglect. Many experts define and redefine the nature of the problem. Often, the distinctions are but a matter of degree and perception.

In our society, there seem to be no groups or sociocultural systems (micro or macro) that have not been contaminated by incidents of childhood maltreatment. Child abuse has been found in youth groups, in our educational system, among personnel in our armed forces, in athletic groups, and in our religious institutions. Whether it occurs in intrafamilial or extrafamilial systems, our nation's children bear the wounds from the horrendous acts perpetrated upon them. Is it really so surprising that within a largely dysfunctional, violent society, child abuse, in one or more of its forms, has become institutionalized?

A child who is abused or who perceives he or she was abused must receive adequate and effective psychological treatment. The millions of children who do not obtain a resolution of the devastating impact of childhood abuse are destined to carry its pernicious psychological baggage with them into adulthood. The very nature of our society demonstrates the disastrous effect of permitting adult

survivors to continue to suffer without appropriate psychotherapeutic intervention. Their internal psychological scarring man-
dates us to deal with their suffering now or become its victims. That
it exists in epidemic proportions dictates that the problem can no
longer be left to run its course. Neither the victim nor the perpetrator can be permitted to go unattended. The manifestations of
this condition permeate the very fiber of our society.

The mental health profession is surprisingly ill-equipped to
deal effectively with this pervasive problem. There are practically
no treatment guidelines that clinicians can use as a comprehensive
tool in assisting them to properly treat the adult victim/survivor of
childhood abuse. The dearth of literature prevents otherwise competent professionals from offering appropriate treatment. It is to
this end that this book is dedicated.

1

What Is Childhood Maltreatment and What Are the Long-Term Aftereffects for Adult Survivors?

INTRODUCTION

An analysis of any type of abuse ordinarily requires a working definition of the term. Failing to provide one may hinder the precision required both to convey the author's message and to permit the reader to conceptualize it.

The following includes some of the best thinking on the definitions of the three primary types of abuse.

DEFINITIONS

Psychological Abuse

Garbarino and colleagues (1986) have had the greatest influence on definitions of psychological abuse. They suggested five forms of behavior generally conceded to constitute psychological maltreatment: rejecting, isolating, terrorizing, ignoring, and corrupting. Hart and colleagues (1987) concluded that the above definition has been well received in that psychological abuse is the core issue in child maltreatment. Vissing and Straus (1991) sought to enlarge the scope of this definition by writing about "verbal/symbolic aggression," which they define as

> a communication intended to cause psychological pain to another person, or a communication perceived as having that intent. The communication act may be active or passive, and verbal or nonverbal. Examples include name calling or nasty remarks (active, verbal), slamming a door or smashing something (active, nonverbal), and stony silence or sulking (passive, nonverbal). [p. 224]

While Vissing and Straus enhance our perspective by discussing the nature of the act, that is, active or passive, verbal or nonverbal, their emphasis on intent raises some difficult questions.

Is the nature of psychological abuse objective or subjective? If the perpetrator meant no harm, but a verbal attack can reasonably be construed as harmful, is this abuse? Can a comment normally viewed or actually intended to be abusive be judged inoffensive because the "victim" did not react adversely to it? Can comments generally considered nonabusive be interpreted otherwise because of the particular psychological state of the listener?

It should be noted that the issue of intent, as stated by Vissing and Straus, is not a factor in our definition. Emotional pain inflicted by the thoughtless act of a perpetrator should not be discarded because the consequences were not fully intended. People are responsible for their behavior; they cannot avoid that responsibility by acting negligently.

Physical Abuse

Physical abuse is any nonaccidental or negligent physical contact that causes physical pain or injury. It is true that our society either encourages or tolerates some forms of corporal punishment of children, such as spanking, for various reasons. The intentional infliction of pain or injury upon a child is never justified. By the above definition, it is clear that such conduct must be considered abusive.

To leave the definition of abuse to society would surely constitute an abandonment of our responsibility as professionals to work within the framework of the current state of psychology. The reality of abuse may be far different from the meaning it has for our neighbors. Deciding that spanking or any other form of physical pain or suffering is abusive need not await cultural approval; it is our responsibility.

Sexual Abuse

Much has been written about childhood sexual abuse. Both the malevolence and implications of this problem, which is of nearly epidemic proportions, mandate that additional attention be paid to this serious issue.

The definition of sexual abuse is extremely important. Operational definitions are used to determine when intervention into the privacy of a home and family is permissible. For the purposes of this book, a clear and precise understanding of the survivor's background is, obviously, of great benefit in the therapeutic process. That purpose cannot be attained unless we use a common definition that describes the problem as it exists.

One of the useful definitions of child sexual abuse includes

> any inappropriate sexual interaction with a child, either physical or nonphysical, and includes attempts to exploit the child sexually. Incest, rape, and sodomy are violent forms of abuse, but exposing body parts, suggestive talk, and subjecting children to degrading sexual innuendo are also abusive. [Weikel and Krupinski 1986, p. 101]

CONTRIBUTING FACTORS

The relationship between the victim and perpetrator ranges from parent to total stranger and extends to everyone in between. Whether the abuse is inflicted by a teacher, family friend, or acquaintance, the impact can be devastating.

The emphasis of this section on contributing factors is primarily the intrafamilial relationship, including sibling abuse. It is the one in which most cases of abuse occur and which is typically the most injurious to the victim.

In conceptualizing a clinical picture of the adult survivor of sexual abuse, it is crucial to understand the factors contributing to the victim's psychological problem. These are presented below:

Sexual Abuse

As in any overview, the following family characteristics of incest are more a composite of many cases than absolutes for every incestuous family. However, in reviewing numerous cases, certain familial attributes predictably emerge.

Isolation is a significant characteristic of incestuous families. They generally exhibit a high degree of physical, psychological, and social isolation. The parents of incest victims rarely have trusted peers or activities that take them outside the home. There appears to be little intimacy with others; they engage in superficial contacts. Frequently, the incest victim is the loner in her classroom. She may, in effect, seek isolation in order to more easily harbor her hated secret. The child is often overprotected by the incestuous offender in a similar effort to protect the secret.

Rigidity is another characteristic that typifies incestuous families. The family structure is commonly rigidly authoritarian and patriarchal. In the home, the father seems aggressive while the mother is viewed as submissive and inadequate. Their marital relationship is generally distant and broken-down; within the family there are inflexible rules and relationship roles. Family controls tend to become even more rigid as the child grows and attempts to reach beyond the family to meet her own expanding social needs. For example, she may not be allowed to participate in after-school activities, spend time at a friend's home, or as adolescence approaches, date. These severely dysfunctional families tend to be unable to deal with change.

There often appears to be a reversal of traditional family structure in the incestuous family; that is, the child acts like a parent and the adult manifests infantile coping mechanisms toward the parental role. The child is frequently burdened with many parental responsibilities for the family. A mother–daughter role reversal is common; the daughter is overly concerned with protecting ("mothering") her own mother, a pattern that motivates keeping the incest a secret.

It has been noted that incest tends to have an intergenerational pattern of transmission and often coexists with other types of childhood abuse or trauma. Often one or both of the parents were sexually, physically, or emotionally abused themselves as children. Some males who were sexually abused externalize their victimization by abusing children in an unconscious effort to resolve their own abusive experiences. They later rationalize their responsibility for the abuse by blaming the victim. Females who were abused as children are more likely to internalize their victimization. They may, as adults, seek abusive partners (modeled after their own abusers) who reinforce their already devalued self-concepts. These women are often unsuccessful at protecting their own children from abuse.

In addition to the dysfunctional traits described above, it has been noted that communication is typically closed and ineffective. Feelings are rarely, if ever, expressed assertively; they are usually covert, indirect, and acted-out or acted-in. These families are extremely ineffective at problem solving. Conflicts are submerged in the process, and the child victim in turn feels responsible for protecting the family. The victim's absolute loyalty, at any price, emanates from fear of the dissolution of the family and anticipated subsequent problems. This responsibility impedes the child's development of autonomy and contributes to a failure of the separation-individuation process. In other words, the abused child's abiding loyalty to incestuous family members takes precedence over autonomy and self-realization.

The mother of these psychopathological family systems is usually characterized as extremely dependent (emotionally and financially), helpless, and passive. The mother–daughter bond in incestuous families is generally weak. Sometimes the mother is suffering from a chronic illness such as depression, and is emotionally absent or withdrawn from the family. She often feels exploited, abused, and manipulated by her husband and may unconsciously use her daughter as a shield to protect herself. As mentioned earlier, a high percentage of incest victims' mothers were physically and/or sexually abused as children. The mother may be so preoccupied protecting her own needs, compensating for her own incestuous experience or present abuse, that she fails to recognize or protect her own child from abuse.

There are instances when the mother is consciously or unconsciously aware of the incest, yet finds herself without the insight or skills to deal with the problem. She may repress or deny her suspicions to protect herself from childhood memories of her own abuse. Sometimes she has a great investment in maintaining the status quo and the appearance of normality in her family. Fear of exposure, humiliation, personal harm, or financial ruin all contribute to increase the mother's inability to protect her child.

The notion that incestuous fathers or stepfathers are highly sexed and aggressive men is generally false. Although some incest offenders may appear extremely domineering and authoritative in their families and homes, most are passive and ineffectual individuals outside the family. Their negative self-concepts, low self-esteem, and general feelings of inadequacy are conducive to their maladaptive behavior, which is destructive to themselves and others.

The incest offender rationalizes his parental responsibility to the daughter in an infantile manner in order to satisfy his own unmet needs for nurturing, companionship, and sexual gratification. He binds his daughter into a self-serving relationship by manipulating her needs for affection, love, and attention.

The child victim of incest is most likely to be the eldest daughter in the family. Most child sexual abuse is initiated by the perpetrator well before the child reaches puberty, typically between the ages of 5 and 9 (Weikel and Krupinski 1986), although some data suggest that the average age of onset of incest is during the latency stage of development, perhaps due to better memory capacity of children of that age. Nevertheless, many cases also involve much younger children (Russell 1984). Though victims of child sexual abuse are often blamed by the perpetrators and others for the incest (referred to as "seductive"), it is never the victims' fault for the incest. They were chosen because they were "handy" and "available" (Sgroi 1988).

The impact of sexual abuse upon boys appears more extensive than that suffered by girls. Walker and colleagues (1988) conclude that

> in addition to the symptoms typically seen in female victims, such as shame, depression, guilt, and inappropriate sexual behavior, Rogers and Terry (1984) have described other issues encountered in the treatment of boy victims, which include: (a) confusion over sexual identity and fears of homosexuality; (b) the tendency of boy victims to reenact their victimization by sexually abusing other children; (c) increased aggressive behavior; and (d) strong denial or minimization of the impact by the boys' parents. [p. 153]

However, further research in this area is still warranted.

Females typically internalize their victimization by exhibiting diminished self-esteem and developing passive, overly compliant personalities. The role reversal previously alluded to often leads to what is called pseudomaturity. The parents inappropriately look to the child to fulfill their needs; the child has the weight of the world on her shoulders. She begins to worry not only about financial problems but also how to keep her father or stepfather away from her. Pseudomaturity has been referred to in the literature as the betrayal of innocence, a false maturity in a child too old for her years.

The child learns to experience the world as unsafe; she must always be able to give what is desired. Her sense of self-esteem and well-being is threatened, as is her ability to trust and to establish healthy relationships with others. She tends to lack her own internal controls and is too willing to please others.

The denial of incest by a child who is asked directly is a most common occurrence. The child will often retract her initial disclosure, even after detailed reporting to appropriate individuals. The child's fear of reprisal, her guilt and confusion, and in many cases, pressure placed upon her in the family, cause this commonly observed ambivalence.

Physical Abuse

Theories abound about factors that contribute to the physical maltreatment of children. The psychological literature is replete with formulae accounting for why parents physically abuse their children. Those authors often denounce other theories as unfounded.

The basis for much of the debate is found in the work of Kempe and colleagues. Their widely known theory (1972) postulates that three components need to be present for physical abuse to occur. There must be a parent with the potential, a child who is perceived as difficult by the parent(s), and a crisis or series of crises.

Other contributing factors appear repeatedly in the relevant literature pertaining to child victims of physical maltreatment.

Parents who physically abuse their children have been found to manifest higher levels of stress from multiple sources and are deficient in coping skills to deal effectively with such stress. Problems such as unemployment, substance abuse, financial difficulties, illness, and marital discord are typically reported as considerably stressful (Gelles 1980). Since these parents are more likely to utilize inadequate problem-solving behaviors, they tend not to alter their circumstances and may in fact increase their levels of stress.

Social isolation often increases the likelihood of maltreatment by parents. The family is cut off from environmental supports, thus increasing the impact of stressful situations on the parents and reducing protection and support for the children.

Low self-esteem is another indicator usually manifested by these parents and cited as a factor in aggressive behavior toward their children. In a psychosocial system in which personal power is linked to one's socioeconomic level, lack of employment, for example, may negatively impact on one's sense of self-worth, resulting in child abuse (Flournoy and Wilson 1991).

Physically abusive parents have been observed as having frustrated dependency needs. This dynamic underlies the concept of role reversal, in which the parents unrealistically expect their child(ren) to satisfy their needs (nurturing, housekeeping, etc.).

An additional characteristic identified as an important component in childhood abuse is impulsivity. Many abusive parents act without conscious thought when punishing their children. Such impulsiveness may well lead to physical abuse when it occurs in a parent with the potential for physical maltreatment.

"Children at risk" is an often-referred-to factor in the literature. In many families certain children are more at risk to be abused than are their siblings. Studies have identified several apparent predictors of abusive treatment. Among these variables are the inability of the primary caretaker (typically the mother), to bond with the child, a child's disability, and the failure of the child to satisfy the parents' expectations. These factors, both objective and subjective, are significantly overrepresented in empirical studies of the cause of abuse (Ammerman 1991).

The risk of abusive behavior by battering parents is increased as an outgrowth of poor parenting skills. Many parents have been denied the opportunity to master adequate parenting skills for a variety of reasons. They may have been the offspring of physically abusive parents themselves, exposed to punitive forms of discipline, or have been raised either without siblings or with one in the same age bracket, effectively denying them an opportunity to develop childrearing skills. Many of these families may also be characterized by high levels of psychological abuse, thereby adding to the overall dysfunctional level of the victim.

Ammerman (1991) posits that the causes of such child physical maltreatment are so unique, complex, and multidimensional, that any one-dimensional review would be inadequate. Nevertheless, he insists that "childrens' characteristics" are not useful indicators of whether a particular child will be abused. The question to be answered is, when do "child factors contribute to the overall likelihood of abuse?" (p. 97).

Psychological Abuse

Perhaps the most difficult form of child abuse to assess in terms of parental contributing factors is that of psychological maltreatment. As previously discussed, it is the most ambiguous to define and yet may be the most common type of abuse inflicted on children by parents, some well meaning. It has even been forcefully suggested that psychological abuse is an integral part of all other types of abuse (Garrison 1987).

Nevertheless, we can usually identify psychological abuse as we find it and can postulate a number of family characteristics that contribute to this insidious form of child maltreatment.

One of the significant factors noted in psychological abuse is maladaptive communication patterns. In this instance, we are referring to ineffective communications in which the family members have difficulty expressing their real feelings and thoughts openly, directly, and respectfully. In some families, children are discouraged from verbally expressing themselves in an adaptive manner, while parents are often verbally aggressive. It is an outgrowth of the too familiar children-should-be-seen-and-not-heard or the no-talk rule.

Dysfunctional patterns are manifested by incongruent, indirect, hidden, and closed types of communication. Also, parents may express themselves verbally in ways that are judgmental, attacking, blaming, and labeling. For example, feelings are evaluated as good or bad, strong or weak, or right or wrong. Some parents present mixed messages to their children, such as smiling when sad. Another type of dysfunctional process is that which places the child in a double bind; he is damned if he does and damned if he doesn't.

In such families, the parents tend to speak for each other and certainly for the child. Expressions are often aggressive and/or passive; the art of being assertive is rarely effectuated. Rather, the child is exposed to verbally passive and/or aggressive parents who are often hostile and fail to resolve conflicts. Verbal projections onto the child(ren) of the parents' ego-alien traits may be commonplace or displaced from the spousal system to the child. The communication system is, in short, too defensive.

Another factor often noted of psychologically abusive families is dysfunctional boundaries. The violation of the child's internal boundaries is an example of psychological abuse. These boundaries, which can be thought of as symbolic fences, permit the child to develop a healthy sense of self and identity. When these boundaries are transgressed and the child becomes either enmeshed or disengaged, the child loses that sense of self. Those rhetorical questions "Who am I?" and "Where do I stand?" remain unanswered. Rather than encountering those necessary firm but flexible boundaries, the child is unable to set age-appropriate limits. The consequences to the child include a lack of awareness of thoughts, feelings, and behavior for which he is responsible. He cannot distinguish between taking responsibility for himself and the extent to which he is responsible for others.

With this form of maltreatment, the child is confronted by parents who blame him for both the feelings and the behavior of the adult. "You made me angry" and "You made me do . . ." echo through the victim's formative years.

Another factor contributing to psychological maltreatment of children is the imposition of rigid family roles. Unlike the structure found in a functional family, abusive family roles are inflexible. Rather than remaining flexible and reflective of the "true self," rigid roles are imposed, not negotiated, and rarely discussed. They are confining in that particular feelings are an integral part of the fixed role, to be inherited by the child(ren) upon whom the role is imposed.

Instead of fitting the role to the child, the youngster is mandated to fulfill the family's needs and expectations. That these roles may be age inappropriate and beyond the child's developmental stage and capacity is inconsequential. The child assumes that the role is who he really is; so are the "star," "caretaker," "scapegoat," and "lost child" born. If the expectations are unrealistic, the child may very well suffer from a loss of self-esteem along with fear of abandonment and rejection.

A frequent reappearing form of mental abuse is the imposition of rigid family rules. Like family "laws," they are inflexible and absolute, though at times unspoken. As with many other kinds of laws, they may be ambiguous, unrealistic, or arbitrary. Predicated neither on discussion nor compromise, they are often unrealistic and outdated.

These rules, by their very nature, are to be complied with, not questioned or challenged. They often inhibit the child(ren) from thinking, feeling, and talking. They leave no latitude to be imperfect; mistakes are not tolerated. Perhaps the most fundamental rule of the abusive family is to keep its secrets.

The prescribed rules frequently deal with the *shoulds* and *oughts* as they regulate the child's decision-making ability and behavior. Victims of these rigid rules are strictly accountable for their adherence; the parents have little, if any, accountability for their formulation. Many are just passed down from generation to generation.

It has also been observed that certain parental personal variables contribute to the psychological maltreatment of children. As is true of other forms of abuse, parents who abuse their children have often themselves been victims of childhood abuse. Because their needs were not satisfied as children, they look to their own children to fill their dependency needs. If the children cannot meet the parents' needs and expectations, the parents feel betrayed and insecure. The children then become the parental scapegoats.

Parents suffering from impulsivity, illness, high stress, and low frustration tolerance may also contribute to psychological maltreatment. Included among other characteristics are witnessing family violence, parental substance abuse, difficulty with problem solving, ineffective and poor parenting skills, and families that tend to function in isolation, lacking support networks (Garbarino et al. 1986).

DEFENSES

Seemingly, most trauma/abuse patients utilize lower and intermediate level defenses. Lower Level Defenses (psychotic) center around the splitting mechanism and include splitting, projections, projection identification, primitive idealization, primitive denial, and negative introjection. Intermediate level defenses include somatization, intellectualization, identification with the aggressor, rationalization, denial, suppression, displacement, and avoidance, among others. Other patients may use a combination of higher level defenses with intermediate level mechanisms. They center around repression, in combination with other neurotic defenses.

LONG-TERM AFTEREFFECTS OF CHILDHOOD ABUSE

Adult survivors are subject to a substantial array of long-term aftereffects of their abuse. Table 1-1 presents a list of many of the typical maladies observed in survivors.

TABLE 1-1.   Long-Term Aftereffects of Childhood
Abuse/Trauma

I. *Distorted Cognitive Schemata*
   Decreased self-confidence
   Distrust of others
   Distorted self/object
      representation
   Lack of empowerment
   Impaired self-esteem
   Decreased sense of safety
   Impaired sense of autonomy
   Impaired capacity for intimacy
II. *Affective (Emotional) Problems*
   Heightened anxiety/
      fears/phobias
   Irrational guilt
   Affective constriction
   Repressed anger/hostility/rage
   Depression
   Panic disorders
   Shame
   Psychic pain/agony/anguish
   Feeling of isolation
   Terror/horror
   Emotional oversensitivity
   Emotional "hardness"
   Sadness/grief/despair
III. *Behavioral Problems*
   Learned helplessness
   Self-destructive behaviors
   Repetition compulsion
   Post-Traumatic Stress Disorder
      reaction symptoms
   Addictions
   Dissociation
   Obsessive thoughts
   Compulsive behaviors
   Amnesia for the events/trauma
   Aggression
   Learning difficulties
   Overachievement/
      underachievement

IV. *Physical Problems*
   Frequent headaches/migraines
   PMS
   Backaches
   Respiratory problems
   Gastrointestinal problems
   Cardiology problems
   Gynecological problems
   Increase in pharmacological
      treatment
   Urinary problems
V. *Sexual Dysfunction/Problems*
   Compulsive sexual behavior
   Desire disorder (aversion to
      sex/low desire)
   Orgasmic disorders
   Arousal disorders
   Sexual pain disorders
   Sexual identity confusion issues
   Sexualized relationships
   Sexual acting out
   Sexual orientation issues
VI. *Interpersonal/Social Problems*
   Fear of intimacy
   Vulnerability to repeat
      victimizations
   Social isolation/alienation
   Difficulty with boundaries—
      self and others
   Social hyperactivity
   Social inactivity
   Marital/couple discord
   Impaired limit-setting abilities
   Deficits in interpersonal skills
   Deficits in coping/life
      management skills
   Antisocial behavior
   Fear of being touched
   Inadequate parenting skills
   Criminal behavior

2

The Adult Clinical Presentation and Assessment of Childhood Abuse

INTRODUCTION

It is critical, when working with adult patients whose history indicates the presence of trauma during the formative years, to conduct a complete clinical evaluation. A description of the presenting symptomatology is frequently not enough to acquire a full understanding of how a particular trauma, whether emotional, physical, or sexual, may have been responsible for the presenting emotional or behavioral dysfunction a person manifests in adult life.

A comprehensive clinical evaluation requires a detailed developmental history and a thorough investigation of the family dynamics, including the cultural and social environment in which the patient developed.

The clinician should sort out intrapsychic from external-environmental factors and, to the fullest extent possible, assess the impact multiple variables and contributing factors have had on the individual's psychological formation. The presenting symptomatology could be the result of several different factors that need to be assessed in conjunction with any perceived emotional, physical or sexual abuse. The evaluator should keep in mind that neglect, rejection, or periods of abandonment during critical developmental stages could be as insidious and as traumatic as any later physical or sexual abuse. Of course, many times they coexist and may disguise each other.

It usually makes a dramatic difference whether the traumatic experience disrupted mental structuring still in formation or already solidified (e.g., cognitive schemata, ego resources, and self capacities). At times, it is impossible to isolate a single traumatic experience as being responsible for all of the patient's dysfunction. Generally, a disruptive experience in early childhood that causes an alteration of the normal developmental currents will have a far-reaching and more profound impact on the future adult than if the traumatic event had taken place in a previously well-adapted, developmentally more advanced child (see cases A and B).

Many of the sexually, emotionally, or physically abused individuals we see in our consulting rooms present signs and symptoms compatible with descriptive diagnoses such as histrionic and borderline personality disorders, which can lead the clinician to an inaccurate understanding and a faulty formulation of the psychodynamics of the problem, even though the descriptive diagnosis may be accurate. In other words, the clinical (descriptive) presentation should not be the only basis for formulating a specific treatment approach. Furthermore, the clinician should avoid arriving at premature, and especially speculative, formulations about the cause of the patient's dysfunction (such as attributing to a faulty parent–child relationship a borderline-type presentation).

When facing a clinical dilemma like this, the clinician/diagnostician might ask herself: In addition to the history of emotional, sexual, or physical abuse at a later age, was this person traumatized as a child? Was he abandoned during critical developmental phases? Was the person able to compensate for early abuse by developing and using healthy ego-adaptive mechanisms? Did the later trauma disrupt the homeostasis completed early on? Is the patient in a temporary regressive state needing only the therapist to enhance the use of previous, successfully used coping mechanisms? How was the patient able to overcome preexisting trauma (if any) and how will the patient be able to recall those healthier defenses? What are the mental structures that have been disrupted or fragmented? What are the ego functions that are affected by the trauma? (Beres [1956] describes ego functions as [1] regulation and control of instinctual drives, [2] relation to reality, [3] object relations, [4] thought processes, [5] defense functions, [6] autonomous functions, and [7] synthetic functions.) Is the patient able to maintain a good reality testing? Is the regulation of self-esteem disrupted by fragmentation of the self or the ego ideal–superego subsystem? Is the patient blaming himself for the traumatic event? Is he severely self-critical? Was the capacity to relate to others more severely affected? Can he get attached? Can he trust others? It is important to clarify questions that arise in the mind of the clinician as the evaluation process goes on.

Taking a longitudinal view of the patient's vicissitudes along his developmental history is extremely helpful in deciding whether the person has been chronically dysfunctional. In other words, is one dealing with a combination of etiological and contributing factors that may require more complex therapeutic interventions (probably the worst clinical scenario)? Or is the patient a previously well-adjusted, functional individual who suddenly became symptomatic, but whose clinical presentation is strikingly similar to that of the previously described, chronically dysfunctional patient?

Obviously, the clinical formulation and recommendations for treatment will be dramatically different from one situation to the other despite the fact that both may share the same descriptive qualities. Here are two examples:

Patient A was a college dropout who decompensated into a severe, psychotic level of functioning following the first separation at college from her parents. The history indicated that Patient A grew up in a chronically dysfunctional family, where mental disorder was suspected in both parents. Patient A had shown separation difficulties since age 3. She demonstrated a better-than-average intellectual capacity and a surprisingly good psychological mindedness. She was treated for many years as a psychotic patient with multiple hospitalizations and the use of heavy dosages of psychotropics. The patient's severe dysfunction was reflected in her extremely poor object relationships and her inability to hold a job or take care of herself. She was emotionally abused and neglected, as she perceived it; at times, she would put herself in situations in which she would run the risk of being sexually exploited and physically abused. In spite of having been raped, she would occasionally walk alone in the middle of the night around areas where she had been victimized before, as if trying to master the trauma. Every time the sexual abuse became the focus of a session, the patient would minimize both its importance and the impact of the experience. She would shrug it off or would not want to talk about it.

It is clear from the description that this particular patient was dealing with her subsequent traumas in a very dysfunctional, maladaptive, and primitive way. That way of coping, however, was the only way she knew, due to her low level of character organization. Her clinical presentation had to be considered in the context of her past severe emotional deprivation. She was not overtly psychotic (even though she was treated as such for several years), but she would very well fit the borderline spectrum of mental disorders. The sexual trauma was an additional, and perhaps not the most important or disruptive, factor in her functioning, but it

This case illustrates the fact that sexual, emotional, or physical abuse can remain latent and clinically silent for many years. There are many individual factors to be taken into account before a decision is made about how to approach a problem in the most effective manner possible. Cases A and B illustrate the dilemma faced by many clinicians and therapists in trying to sort out and formulate the important etiological factors, especially in the presence of behavioral and intrapsychic dysfunction, when there is a history of emotional, sexual, or physical abuse in the patient at an early or later stage in life (see Figures 2-1, 2-2, and 2-3). Viewing the mere presence of emotional, sexual, or physical

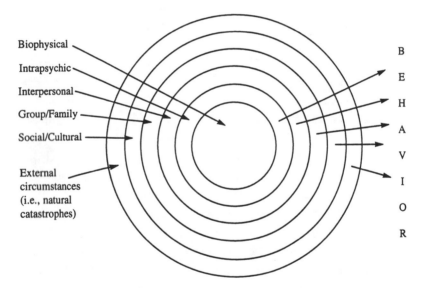

Figure 2-1 illustrates the different factors that contribute to individual behavior whether normal or pathological, adaptive or maladaptive. Copyright © 1994 Francisco Cruz, Laura Essen, and Carlos Estrada. Courtesy of Carlos Estrada.

had to be dealt with in conjunction with her other multiple problems.

Patient B was a college graduate in her thirties, very attractive and intellectually endowed. Her premorbid history described a well-adjusted, high-functioning individual. Following her college graduation, she obtained a well-paid job that consisted mostly of advocating for the victims of social ills and injustices. She would help poor people, the mentally ill, and other victims, to get proper help or adequate mental treatment. She became symptomatic and was diagnosed as suffering severe anxiety episodes after several years of successful work. It became increasingly clear that the underlying conflict was a reactivation (perhaps through her daily exposure to similar experiences in others) of an early sexual abuse and repeated mental manipulation and extortion by her biological father. Her anxiety attacks exacerbated when she tried to formalize a relationship with her boyfriend and became aware of her sexual inhibitions. Underlying and feeding her emotional conflicts was her intense fear of, and lack of enjoyment of, sexual relationships. These fears and inhibitions later on in treatment turned into rage as she realized and recovered the repressed memories of the sexual abuse and how she had been scarred by her father from age 4 through age 6.

The uncovering and further explorations of the early seduction and subsequent trauma, the recovery of the memories of the events and details of the above, the consultation about and the understanding of her current sexual dysfunction and anxiety attacks in the context of the disruptive experience collectively resulted in a marked decrease of her presenting symptoms and a higher level of functioning different areas of her life, and improvement in her capacity relate to her boyfriend in an intimate sexual way.

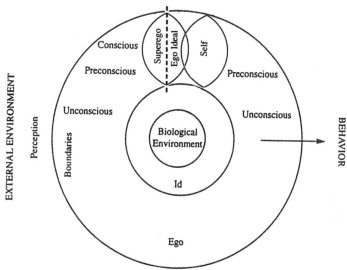

Figure 2-2 is a model of the mind mediating external stimuli and resulting in normal (or abnormal), adaptive (or maladaptive) behavior if mediation of factors (illustrated in Figure 2-1) maintains homeostasis. Copyright © 1994 Francisco Cruz, Laura Essen, and Carlos Estrada. Courtesy of Carlos Estrada.

abuse as the most important area to be dealt with, isolated from any other contributing psychological factors, is as undesirable as taking the position that only patients with character deficiencies become symptomatic in the face of such a history of abuse.

Figure 2-3 illustrates how pervasive and fragmenting a trauma can be to the mental apparatus, affecting different mental structures. As shown, fragmentation of the superego and the ego ideal might be such that it results in a lack of regulation of self-esteem, a tendency to self-blame, and a variety of clinical symptoms such as depression, rigidities, and inhibitions, which frequently are related to superego and ego ideal system dysfunctions. By cutting across the conscious layer of the mind, the trauma

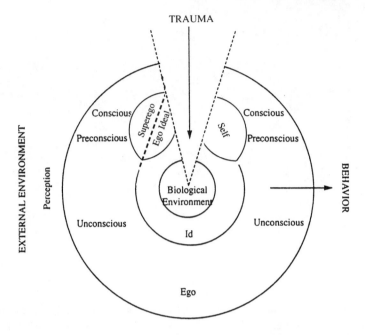

Figure 2–3 shows a model of the mind where mediation is abnormal due to fragmentation of the subsystems of the mind caused by a traumatic disorganizing experience. Copyright © 1994 Francisco Cruz, Laura Essen, and Carlos Estrada. Courtesy of Carlos Estrada.

as illustrated would contaminate primary and secondary process thinking; indeed, the patient may experience uncontrollable aggressive and/or libidinal impulses coming from the repressed, id-related layer of the mind.

The ego would also be fragmented. The clinical manifestation of ego weakness will depend on (1) the severity of the trauma; (2) how advanced the ego is in its developmental process, and (3) how well integrated the ego is. Generally, the less consolidated and primitive the ego structure at the time of the trauma, the more pervasive the ego dysfunctions. The clinical symptoms to be expected from a weak and fragmented ego would be defense mechanisms such as splitting, projection, projective identification, primitive idealization, and primitive denial, among others. Ego dysfunction generally translates into poor interpersonal relationships, and an incapacity to tolerate situations of anxiety and stress and to control impulses. The Self also will be fragmented, and the manifestation of this fragmentation again will be related to how well-developed and consolidated that structure is.

Overall, a variety of clinical symptoms, depending on which structure of the mind was more severely affected, should be expected. Generally, the pockets of dysfunction should be readily identifiable through the evaluation process. The maladaptive or symptomatic behavior observable in the clinical situation may impact different spheres of the mind including the biophysical, intrapsychic, interpersonal, intrafamilial, and social and cultural, as illustrated in Figure 2–4. How the individual copes with unpredictable external circumstances will also be affected by a traumatic event. The treatment modality to be used to correct the structural deficit or dysfunction would have to address the specific areas of the mind that have been affected. The treatment interventions would have to match the area of major dysfunctions. In general terms, this requires a combination of treatment modality that may go from the use of medication to individual, couples, group, or family therapy.

We explore below the different components of the individual to be observed by the clinician.

1. *Biophysical.* This assessment examines biological/physical systems and what they may contribute to the patient's current dysfunction. Is there any genetic predisposition to emotional disorder, such as a history of bipolar illness or schizophrenia among the patient's relatives? Is there any concurrent physical disorder that may be contributing to emotional distress (physical deformity, endocrine disorder, and so on)? The clinician should have an idea

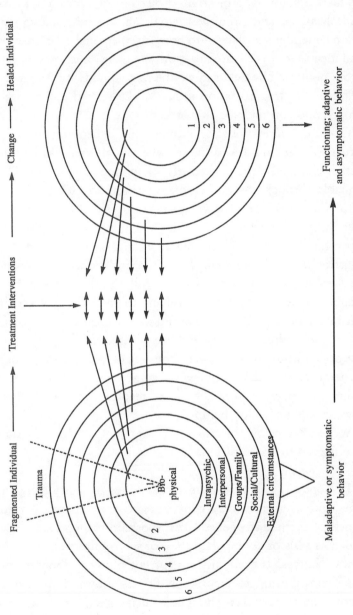

Figure 2–4 is a model of how the clinical intervention can foster changes in the fragmented individual and how the changes, primarily intrapsychic and interpersonal, translate into healthier functioning. Copyright © 1994 Francisco Cruz, Laura Essen, and Carlos Estrada. Courtesy of Carlos Estrada.

about how instinctual drives (libido, aggression, self-preservation) are handled by the individual.

2. *Intrapsychic.* The subject of this assessment would be the mind itself, which includes intelligence, perception, identity, control, memory capacity, and so on. These are areas that should be evaluated.

3. *Interpersonal.* This area deals with how the individual relates, for example, to others, to self, to authority; the quality of object relationships, which includes relating to things, and to animals.

4. *Group/Family.* Questions commonly asked are, What role(s) does the individual take in groups? Is he a leader or a follower? Does he associate or is he usually isolated? How does he function in the matrix of the family and family dynamics? What are the childrearing practices in his family? What roles does he play in the family? What is the quality of those roles?

5. *Social.* Issues about the individual's social stratum, roles, and relationships are important to clarify. What is the patient's experience with interracial and intergenerational relationships? How does the patient relate with different age groups and in sexual relationships?

6. *Cultural.* Belief systems, language problems, ethnicity, religious ideas, ethics, and moral values are also important areas to be assessed.

The goal of a comprehensive clinical assessment is to clarify how the traumas have altered or impacted any of these areas of functioning. The objectives and methods of treatment and intervention should be based on all the variables mentioned above, always attempting to keep an integrated view of the individual.

The table below is an aid for the clinician in the process of gathering pertinent historical material during the evaluation process.

TABLE 2–1.   The Data Gathering Process

Some Pertinent General Questions

When you were a child/adolescent, who was living in the home with you? Who was the primary caretaker? Who was the primary disciplinarian? Were you ever left alone? Where? How often? How old were you? Describe how you felt. How did you deal with that situation? Did you feel overprotected? Underprotected? By whom? Can you describe your relationship with your Mom prior to age 5? Between 6 and 10? 10 and 15? 15 and 19? With Dad? Siblings? Significant others? What kind of expectations did your Mom, Dad (significant others) have of you? What happened if you did something Mom and Dad thought was wrong? What happened if you did something Mom or Dad thought was good? How was affection expressed to you by your Mom, Dad, and significant others?

Questions about Physical Abuse

Did Mom/Dad or significant other(s) discipline you? What method of discipline? Who was involved? How often? For how long? When did it happen? How did you feel? What did you do? Did anyone help you? Did you tell anyone? How did others react? Did it ever consist of corporal punishment? Did Mom or Dad or a significant other ever hit, slap, or spank you? What part(s) of the body? Did it leave marks? Injury? Did they ever kick, pinch, squeeze, or shove you? Leave any marks? Cause any injury? Was there any punching, biting, scratching? Did it leave any marks? Cause any injury? Did you ever have any broken bones or bleeding? Did anyone ever use any object to cause you pain and/or injury?

Questions about Emotional Abuse

Did your Mom/Dad or significant others ever do the following to you? Did your Mom, Dad, siblings, or significant others ever call you names? Did they swear at you? Put you down? Were you the object of jokes and insults? Were your feelings ignored? Did they reject you? Did they humiliate you? Did they tease you? Were there threats of retribution? Did they question your sanity? Did they terrorize or bully you? Did they isolate you from others? Did they routinely tell you you were wrong? Did they tell you that you were bad, unworthy, or not important? Did they ignore you or demand all your attention? Did they not respond to your needs? Did you have to care for their needs? Did they protect you from physical or emotional attacks from others?

(continued)

TABLE 2-1. (continued)

Questions about Sexual Abuse

When you were a child/adolescent, did any parent or significant other ever touch, fondle, hold, or kiss you inappropriately? Force you to touch or look at his or her private parts? Force you to have any sexual contact or activities with him or her? Did any parent or adult ever show you pornographic pictures or films? Tell you explicit sexual stories, jokes, or behaviors? Were you ever forced to be nude or nude with others? Did anyone allow you to be sexually molested? Did anyone manipulate or force you in mutual masturbation? Did anyone ever rape you? Did anyone manipulate or force you to behave in a provocative manner? After toddlerhood, were you made to share your parents' bed? Did they give you enemas when not necessary?

If the patient answered yes to any of the above questions, follow-up should be: By whom? How often? Duration? Where did this happen? How old were you? How did you feel? How did you react? What did you do? Did anyone help you? Did you tell anyone? How did others react when you told them? What did they do?

THE EVALUATION ALLIANCE

Before the clinician engages in the treatment process, it is crucial to develop an evaluation alliance with the patient; the patient should have confidence in the assessment process and in the clinician. The alliance should result in a better capacity to share intimate, detailed information about the past in an atmosphere of honest and open interchange of thoughts and feelings. The clinician should avoid making any premature interpretation or arriving at formulations early in the evaluation process that could interfere with the free flow of psychological material.

The patient should have a clear idea from the start about initial goals of the assessment process and, optimally, should be encouraged to openly verbalize questions or doubts that may come up during its initial phases. Most patients are not aware of all the complexities and intricate aspects of the assessment and how delicately the psychological material needs to be handled.

Patients very frequently expect fast, concrete answers to their problems. The clinician should resist the temptation to jump into a quick explanation of etiology to assuage a patient's demands and expectations. The formulation of the psychodynamics underlying the symptoms should be presented at the appropriate time, when the patient is most receptive to and capable of using it in a therapeutic way. At times, it is difficult to ascertain all the different variables that combined to make the individual symptomatic, and it is not until the person is actually engaged in treatment that other important memories or contributors can be uncovered.

A skilled clinician can afford to use interpretation as part of the evaluation tools and as a well-preconceived strategy to uncover additional material or simply to assess how the patient reacts and handles psychological intervention of this nature.

A cautious, conservative approach in terms of withholding intervention of an interpretative nature usually produces the best results in the long run. The clinician/evaluator should use much tact and empathy when inquiring into the patient's different life experiences, ideals, and vicissitudes.

Intrapsychic Factors

At the end of the diagnostic evaluation, the clinician should be able to ask and answer for herself any question she may have connected with the patient's developmental vicissitudes and resulting character structure. Such questions would be: How far along the developmental spectrum was the patient able to go? Was the trauma a factor in disrupting a specific developmental phase and, if so, how crucial was it? How well has the patient negotiated the separation-individuation process? How does the patient handle interpersonal relationships? Are they conflict-laden? Did the patient achieve object constancy? How does the patient relate to himself? Is the patient harshly self-critical or grandiose? What are the patient's patterns of defensive operations? Does he use primitive or healthy psychological defenses?

These and many other questions and issues should be clear in the mind of the clinician. The material will unfold during the evaluation process if the patient was able to develop a good alliance with the evaluator.

The quality of the interaction with the clinician right from the start will give very valuable clues to the quality of past internalized relationships. Situations such as early idealization or devaluation of the clinician, the use of splitting or other primitive defenses like projection or projective identification, are clearly indicative of an ego that may have failed in its integration process, reflecting a primitive character structure (and it is quite frequent in patients with a history of trauma) or an ego that has defensively regressed to a level of functioning below its actual capacity in the past due to acute anxiety, stress, or trauma.

A patient who is capable of seeing both sides of the coin and is able to temper anger and rage by looking at the positive aspects of the other person most likely is better integrated and may have reached the so called object-constancy stage, according to Mahler and colleagues (1975). The achievement of that developmental milestone will reflect a person with a higher level of functioning, perhaps healthier defenses, and better-quality interpersonal relationships.

The traumatic experience should be seen in the context of very complex and overlapping developmental lines, and to whatever extent possible, the impact of the abuse should be measured in terms of how it affected crucial developmental stages and how the developmental arrest now translates into psychological symptoms (in the case of an abused child) or measured against good premorbid adjustment (in the case of the adult abused as an adult). In other words, the same trauma theoretically may affect the same individual differently depending on the timing of the abuse and the particular developmental current impacted. All these factors combined will give the shape and color to the clinical presentation, and will guide the therapist in choosing appropriate individualized treatment.

A totally different clinical situation is present when dealing with victims of abuse who had a rather good premorbid adjustment and whose history indicates a lack of an early childhood arrest and who have remained asymptomatic until the abuse took place in adolescence or early adulthood. This situation creates a diagnostic challenge for the clinician since the presenting symptoms could very well mimic any other descriptive diagnosis such as a borderline or histrionic disorder (Briere 1989). Only with a continuous refining and adjusting of the patient's account, the quality of the interaction with the examiner, and the evolving clinical process will the therapist have a clear understanding of the etiology of the dysfunction and be able to differentiate it from a preexisting, latent, ready-to-manifest developmental deficit. The question of whether the fragmenting impact of a severe trauma in adolescence or early adulthood has operated in isolation from other psychological factors will be answered only by sorting out all the complex variables and what actually unfolds in the treatment process.

Environmental or External Factors

We refer here to factors predominately alien to the patient's developmental history. It can be argued that any external (social, intrafamilial, groups, and so on) contributor has the potential of being internalized, thus rendering the differentiation between internal and external meaningless. However, for the purpose of the initial clinical assessment, it is valuable for the clinician to sort out the different sources of conflict. How has the individual coped with intrafamilial tension and conflict? How much of a familial dysfunction was absorbed and how much was transformed into a latent or manifested conflict? There are many other questions the clinician may want answers to, to feel satisfied regarding external factors. Some possible questions:

Were there any catastrophic events in the life of the patient, such as a natural disaster that may have created a sudden disruption in the patient's mental homeostasis? How was the nuclear/extended family affected by the awareness of emotional, physical, or sexual abuse? Was there a disruption of the family leading to divorce or separation? Did the abuse take place in a sociocultural environment in which that type of situation can be called endemic? In other words, was it viewed as something to be tolerated?

Again, the border between the external and the intrapsychic is at times blurry and frequently depends on how it is perceived by the victim. For instance, there are patients who are guilt-ridden and constantly blame themselves for their own trauma, thus showing a psychological cloudiness regarding the source of the trauma.

Adjunctive Assessment Tools

The use of adjunctive diagnostic tools such as psychological testing, and neurological and medical tests and assessment could be part of a comprehensive diagnostic process if a clinical condition is suspected. Projective testing is very useful, particularly to differentiate underlying psychotic disorder, and can also give the clinician an idea about how much potential for disorganization of thought may exist in a particular patient. Knowing that the patient has no other neurological or medical condition should make the clinician more confident that what is at issue is a pure psychological disorder. These adjunctive tools are at times not clinically necessary or indicated and must not take the place of a good clinical interview.

FINAL FORMULATION, DIAGNOSIS AND TREATMENT RECOMMENDATION

The last stage of the assessment process has to do with the organization of all psychological and medical data and formulating and presenting it to the patient in a coherent, helpful manner that stimulates further curiosity and motivation to learn. The clinician should judge carefully how much the patient ought to know to avoid overintellectualizing the psychological material.

The patient should be allowed to inquire, question, and challenge any of the psychological material. There should be a free flow of communication and an interchange of ideas preceding the issue of treatment alternatives. The treatment recommendation should be heavily based on the dynamic and diagnostic assessments and not necessarily on the presenting symptoms; needless to say, the dynamic issues will be different from patient to patient, even though the history and description of the abuse may be similar. The treatment should be individualized in terms of uncovered, internalized conflicts, keeping always in mind the impact of the traumatic experience. It is not necessary always to focus just on the trauma itself unless it has occurred in isolation and in a context of good premorbid functioning.

In other words, as the complexities of the past or recent injuries are dealt with in conjunction with the way they impacted on structural development or current functioning, the patient will gradually become less symptomatic and better integrated.

From the results of the diagnostic evaluation it becomes clear that either the premorbid functioning (in the case of well-adjusted individuals) or the underlying character pathology will dictate the optimum individualized treatment approach needed. The same physical, emotional, sexual abuse not only will manifest differently in a low-level personality structure versus a neurotic-level functioning patient or a premorbidly well-adjusted person, but the technical approach should be substantially different. The potential for regressive behavior, the presence of an observing ego, the quality of defense operations, the capacity for attachment, and the development of the therapeutic alliance are only some of the issues that will manifest in different ways and intensity depending upon the patient's different character structure, developmental history, and premorbid adjustment.

PRACTICAL ISSUES PRIOR TO BEGINNING TREATMENT

How frequently should the therapy sessions be? For how long? Should the patient need pharmacotherapy, how will the therapist communicate with the physician? How confidentially should the material be kept from other therapists? How does the patient feel about that? Is the patient's treatment being paid for by parents? If marital or family therapy is indicated, how are all therapists kept aware of the patient's struggles and progress?

There are many questions and issues the therapist should try to clarify before entering into a therapeutic contract to avoid misunderstanding and contamination of the process, as conflicts unfold.

Since most adult survivor patients do not disclose their abuse history during the intake or initial stage of treatment, the following Patient Intake Form, Table 2–2 (see pages 34–35), will assist the clinician during the data gathering process in the appropriate areas to be explored.

TABLE 2–2. Patient Intake Form

I. Patient Intake Information
   A. Identifying date
   B. Medical questionnaire
      1. Past
      2. Present
II. Presenting Problem
   A. Presenting symptomatology with onset, duration, and precipitating factors
      1. Physical
      2. Cognitive
      3. Emotional
      4. Behavioral
      5. Interpersonal
   B. Effects on work/school functioning
   C. Effects on role(s) functioning
      1. Family relationships
      2. Peer relationships
      3. Other relationships
   D. Effects on independent living
   E. What brings patient into therapy at the present time?
   F. How has the patient dealt with the problem so far?
III. Psychosocial History
   A. Pre-abuse development
   B. Post-abuse development
   C. Family history
      1. Relationships with nuclear family members—quality of each
      2. Relationshps with extended family members—quality of each
      3. Description and quality of parents' relationship
      4. Psychiatric history
   D. History of significant others
      1. Peer relationships—quality of each
      2. Other significant relationships—quality of each
   E. School/Education history
   F. Employment history
   G. Psychiatric history
   H. Military history
   I. Past drug/alcohol abuse or other addictions
   J. Past losses/separations/accidents/ or revictimizations
      1. Who? When? What? How? Why?
      2. What coping behaviors employed?
      3. How successful were they?

(continued)

TABLE 2-2. (Continued)

IV. Adult Adjustment
   A. Mental status exam
   B. Current role(s) — level of functioning and achievements
   C. Current relationships — quality of each
   D. Recreational activities, hobbies, sports, interests, etc.
   E. Current psychosocial stressors
      1. Family
      2. Social
      3. Employment/schoolwork-related
      4. Financial
      5. Physical
      6. Other?
   F. Present drug/alcohol/abuse or other additions
   G. Ego strengths
   H. Ego deficits
   I. Feelings about self and others
   J. Revictimizations
   K. Current military status
   L. Patient's strengths and limitations
V. Psychotherapeutic Status
   A. Voluntary or involuntary
   B. Motivation
   C. Opportunity
   D. Capacity
   E. Expectations of therapy
   F. Relatedness to clinician
   G. Prior psychotherapy

3

The Therapeutic Matrix

The adult survivor of childhood abuse who is undergoing psychotherapy is usually hesitant to disclose painful secrets and feelings. The initial task of the clinician should be to create and maintain a safe and secure therapeutic environment free from experiences that in any way would be exploitative or that could revictimize the patient.

A vital task of the clinician lies in the building of a meaningful therapeutic relationship with the patient. The bonding process has aspects both common and unique, as compared with therapy for patients suffering from other types of emotional disorders. Clearly, without keen sensitivity to and careful awareness of the unique characteristics of these patients, the psychotherapeutic process will most likely be ineffective. The importance of the relationship to be developed is emphasized by Perlman (1979), who describes it as "a catalyst, an enabling dynamism in the support, nurture and freeing of people's energies and motivation toward problem solving and the use of help" (p. 2).

Although the therapeutic ingredients involved in bonding may seem immediately obvious and comprehensible, on closer examination the complexity of their nature becomes apparent. The following qualities of the clinician are generally believed to be requisites for developing a therapeutic alliance with the adult survivor of abuse.

THE THERAPIST'S CONTRIBUTION TO THE THERAPEUTIC ALLIANCE

The effective psychotherapist needs to consistently and reliably convey empathy and interest in the patient. The importance of genuineness, acceptance, and openness cannot be overemphasized. There must be a healthy mixture between honesty and empathy. Buber defined the connection as an "I–Thou" relationship in which the individuality and humanness of the patient is recognized and valued. The clinician must be attentive and responsive.

This places demands on the therapist to be emotionally stable and consistent, and to model self-control moderated by flexibility, spontaneity, and a sense of humor. Naturally, the clinician's individual way of thinking, feeling, and talking must convey sincerity and congruence. To the extent that the therapist can draw upon a wide repertoire of knowledge, wisdom, skill, and experience, goals will become more attainable.

The therapist's ability to try to share and resonate with both the patient's emotional pain and vicissitudes will give the patient a unique opportunity, which could be corrective in itself, to realize that others can understand and see his or her problems from the same perspective.

The patient's perception of the therapist as a benign, understanding figure puts the treater in a vantage position and surely will make any therapeutic intervention more effective. But the empathic position of the therapist is not to be confused with supportive interventions or an open display of warmth or caring behavior on the part of the therapist. To be empathic does not mean to verbalize to the patient that one is aware of or shares the patient's emotional pain; it is closer to being capable of using one's emotional attunement to the patient to formulate an intervention that the patient ultimately will identify as truly fitting his inner conflict. In other words, empathy will serve as a facilitator of whatever intervention the therapist deems necessary at a given time. It gives the therapist a vantage point into the therapeutic dialogue.

THE IMPORTANCE OF TRUST

Trust is considered the keystone of the therapeutic relationship with traumatized patients. Only on experiencing a trusting alliance with the therapist will the adult survivor feel safe enough to begin the arduous journey toward healing. The patient's history, frequently filled with memories of rejection and abandonment, will at times make trusting the therapist a difficult task.

Patients usually feel vulnerable and anticipate rejection, abandonment, separation or loss, disillusionment, and betrayal. The intensity of those feelings correspondingly intensifies the complexities often associated with the therapist–patient relationship. It is widely recognized that patients will tend to anticipate and, sometimes re-create past dysfunctional relationships in which mistrust and betrayal predominated. Mistrust, therefore, can be a major source of resistance among adult survivors who come from a background of familial or other interpersonal relationships that have resulted in their being repeatedly betrayed, though this problem is not exclusive to this population.

Some patients may relate to the treater as they would to a parent or authority figure. They may become fearful of being harmed or exploited by the therapist. Their devalued self-concept and identification with the role of victim, together with their sense of powerlessness, increases their fear of betrayal. These patients frequently feel ignored and unlovable. Their hearts and spirits have been unprotected or neglected so that they have been made to feel unworthy of care. A trusting relationship is one of the indispensable building blocks in working with them.

It is essential that the therapist unwaveringly offer this vital therapeutic matrix over the entire course of treatment, no matter how rigorously tested by the patient. It is hoped that this consistency, and the positive relationship it engenders, will promote the ability of the adult survivor to establish other healthy, meaningful, and intimate relationships.

BARRIERS TO TREATMENT

A safe, secure, and dependable atmosphere must be established to reinforce a positive alliance and cut through the therapeutic barriers often present with these patients. According to Herman (1981), some of the barriers to establishing a positive working relationship with the adult survivor "are the same problems that often lead the patient to seek help in the first place: her feelings of shame and hopelessness, and her fear of betrayal in intimate relationships" (p. 189). The patient's probing of the therapist's consistency and commitment must be recognized as a significant and pervasive issue for the patient to work through and should not be taken personally by the therapist.

It is imperative for successful treatment that the clinician convey a sense of belief in the survivor's disclosures. Since these patients typically feel guilty and responsible for the abuse they have suffered, the therapist should clearly convey the message that the patient is believed now, thus helping the patient to begin to ameliorate cognitive distortions.

Although the therapist demonstrates acceptance and a non-judgmental attitude toward the patient on hearing about her often secret past, the adult survivor of childhood abuse may still have intense feeling of shame that keep her from returning for further treatment.

While forming this therapeutic alliance it is necessary to convey to the patient that what happened is not her fault, that the perpetrator, not the patient, is accountable for the abuse. Obviously, as a child the patient did not have the capacity to seduce anyone or to arouse uncontrollable anger in an individual functioning on an adult level. Hearing this from a professional will generally reduce the patient's sense of guilt and any feelings of being bad or unworthy; it will likely aid in the development of a healthier and more positive self-esteem and self-concept. At times it is reassuring for the patient to hear from the clinician of past successes in treating other survivors with similar histories and problems. Helping patients understand the profound problem of abuse within our society via a psychoeducational approach will enable a patient to begin to build a sense of self-acceptance and hope. Additionally, the wall of isolation surrounding her will start to crumble as she feels a sense of commonality with the vast number of others similarly affected.

OTHER THERAPEUTIC FACTORS

Several goals for treating these patients are common to all therapeutic processes. These include:

1. To be available and predictable as a helping, benign figure
2. To encourage ventilation of feelings in a noncritical atmosphere
3. To foster in patients the capacity to sustain themselves by internalizing the helping figure of the therapist
4. To avoid placing the therapist's gratification on the basis of patient progress or the outcome of the treatment
5. To consistently encourage adaptive behavior
6. To be able to keep in check the therapist's emotional reaction to the patient and make therapeutic use of countertransference
7. To help patients become more integrated and able to accept both their strengths and limitations.

TRANSFERENCE

When working with adult survivors of childhood abuse, it is essential to have a heightened awareness of transference reactions and an understanding of the phenomenon. One must constantly monitor what, why, how, and when responses are being influenced by this process in ways that are having an impact on the patient and the therapeutic relationship.

Transference—the projection of previous attitudes, feelings, ideas, and reactions onto the therapist in the current relationship is an unconscious recreation of an earlier object relationship. Patients respond as if the clinician were their mother, father, sister, brother, or some other significant other from childhood. These transferences can result in feelings of love, hate or ambivalence, and the effect on the therapeutic process will depend on how they are handled by the therapist.

Because traumatized patients probably have had many negative interactions, such as maltreatment and rejection, with significant others, it is likely they will anticipate such behavior from some of the people that they encounter. Accordingly, the therapist can expect to become a subject of such a maladaptive assumption. With this in mind, the therapist may find it helpful to work on the patient's distorted perceptions.

The following case illustrates the development of a transference reaction:

> This patient was an attractive woman in her mid-twenties with a history of having been sexually molested by her biological father for many years from the time she was 3. The patient had recently broken up a dysfunctional love relationship in which she played the role of the rescuer. Frequently, she found herself trying to protect and defend her boyfriend from legal, financial, and emotional difficulties. The patient was a talented young professional who devoted most of her time to helping and working with socially and emotionally deprived

people. At times she gave the impression that she was projecting her own deprived self onto her boyfriend and had taken care of her own needs vicariously through him. It took her some time to realize that this person she idealized was, in fact, taking advantage of her in many ways. At that point she made the painful decision to break up the relationship. The breakup was precipitated by his participating in illegal activities and her fear of getting involved in his antisocial behavior.

Not too long after the breakup the patient discussed meeting a man at work. She described a situation very similar to the one that led to the involvement with the previous boyfriend and she announced that she had decided to get married. She was very angry at her stepfather and mother for not being supportive of the relationship, and for being reluctant to attend the wedding ceremony. On further exploration of her need to become impulsively involved in a relationship with somebody she hardly knew, she began to perceive the therapist as a judgmental, critical person, much as she perceived her stepfather and her mother. She was very verbal, expressing her anger and disappointment and what appeared to have been an accumulated negative perception of the therapist. She unleashed a massive explosion of negative feelings and anger. At a deeper level her rage was connected to her mother, who allowed the abuse from her biological father to take place at an early age and who did nothing to stop her suffering. It took several sessions to help her see the distortion in her perception of the therapist and how she was clearly transferring feelings and perceptions she had of her internalized parental figures.

Splitting and Projective Identification

The psychotherapist is often perceived in dramatically contradictory ways by the patient; this may fluctuate between "bad parent" and "good parent" images. These patients try to force the therapist into playing the role of the rejecting abusive parent or project an idealized, longed-for, all good fantasy parent, repeatedly playing out their former (real or fantasized) relationships with the therapist.

At times the patient exercises so much pressure on the therapist to identify with the role being projected on him that the therapist's behavior during the therapy session becomes a replica of the internalized object representation with all its affective components. The therapist's behavior then fits the patient's preconceived idea of him. The result of the re-creation of this early pathological object relationship could be devastating to the treatment process if not actively interpreted and worked through.

By the same token, the therapist ought to be aware of the patient's tendency to cast him in an idealized role. If identified with that role the therapist would become overly involved, the "rescuer"—too supportive or too caring. This situation is also likely to have a negative outcome. Being aware of this dynamic affords the therapist a rich opportunity to begin to titrate his intervention, allowing for the further growth of the therapeutic relationship, which as a by-product will be nurturing and supportive. Obviously, a therapist cannot make up for what patients missed from their natural parents, but the therapist can certainly provide a safe matrix in which patients may see their potential for growth unfold.

The following case illustrates the use of projective identification:

> The patient was a chronically ill female in her late twenties who had been in and out of psychiatric hospitals for several years. She had a history of emotional abuse and neglect at an early age and sexual abuse in her twenties. The patient had a severe borderline disorder and had experienced several psychotic episodes in the past. The patient's relationship with the therapist was dominated by wide fluctuations in her perception, characterized by splitting, projection and projective

identification. There were times where the therapist was idealized and perceived as the only person that had ever understood her problem and who had ever made an effort to listen to her. This was contrasted with the opposite perception of the therapist as being a sadistic, depriving, unconcerned person, unprepared to deal with her problem.

She accused her parents repeatedly of being inconsistent, unpredictable, and unreliable. She would test the therapist to the limit to see if he was going to treat her as she had always been treated, in an inconsistent, contradictory manner. She would cancel appointments and then call at odd hours of the night to let the therapist know how depressed and empty she was feeling. She would complain about his lack of skills in handling her case or would accuse him of intentionally trying to hurt her in a sadistic way. Her therapy was a painful, frustrating process that began to bear fruit only after a year of twice-weekly sessions. She would exercise pressure in the interaction in an attempt to provoke a negative reaction in the therapist; and she would, at times, in a very graphic way, share what she would do to the therapist if she had the chance to inflict pain on him. The patient was able to realize that the therapist could contain his own negative reaction. She felt reassured that she could not destroy the therapist; her display of aggression would not diminish his interest in helping her.

All this material was interpreted as her need to project the negative internalized experiences onto the therapist as a way of relieving her inner tension. By not identifying with her projection the therapist gave the patient not only a sense of relief but time to metabolize and better understand the origin of her distortion. At the same time it gave the patient the opportunity to take in a more supportive and understanding figure that would later translate into a higher functioning and better integrated ego. This proved to be the case as she entered her second year of therapy.

Transference Phenomena in the Therapeutic Environment

Childhood experiences of betrayal, exploitation, abandonment, rejection, and manipulation are typically reexperienced and transferred to therapists in all kinds of therapeutic processes, regardless of the treater's theoretical framework.

It is essential that the transference be handled in such a way that it does not become a stumbling block. In spite of the efforts by the clinician to be genuinely caring and empathic, the patient may unconsciously anticipate that the therapist will take advantage of her to meet the therapist's own needs in a way the patient has experienced before. Briere (1989) states clearly,

> It is, therefore, quite important that the clinician not respond to transferential behaviors as if they were really directed at him or her but, instead, view them as samples of the survivor's understanding of himself and others. The therapist who, for example, responds to rageful behaviors from her client with angry or punitive behaviors of her own is likely to recapitulate the original abuse context and, thereby, reinforce the survivor's belief that her victimizations-base assumptions are correct. [p. 70]

Of course, a therapist reacting this way is being dominated by his or her own countertransference fed by projective identification. These negative transference and countertransference reactions can be utilized in a therapeutic way to examine and clarify past object relationships.

It is critical during these arduous interactions that the therapist continue to provide a trusting, predictable, and reliable relationship that allows patients to modify their "bad," internalized, pathological object relationship, which, in the long term, will translate into psychological growth. Patients will ultimately develop the capacity for self-soothing and containing their emotional turmoil.

Facilitating the Discharge of Aggression

The therapist frequently becomes the focus of the patient's feelings of anger and rage, reactivated in the context of the therapy process.

Sometimes the anger is not only reactivated by undesirable memories from the past but is also fed by a negative patient–therapist transference reaction. If this situation occurs, the clinician should try to explore it with the patient and understand it by going from the present to the past via clarification and interpretation. Otherwise, the patient is likely to feel revictimized and may prematurely terminate treatment.

Clearly, it is essential during the course of treatment to recognize, evaluate, comprehend, and discuss not only the patient's transferential anger but also any reality-based feelings of anger. The psychotherapist can be a positive role model during these interactions by listening, empathizing, and, at times, metabolizing together the patient's anger.

Patients desperately need the opportunity to share their anger with someone who will not respond negatively. Given the probability that many adult survivors were overtly or covertly discouraged or punished as children for expressing their real feelings, it is desirable to give clearly stated permission for them to express their feelings, especially anger, irritation, and annoyance, knowing they will be listened to, respected, and responded to appropriately.

The therapist must then deal with the anger without personalizing it and convey the message that the expression of appropriate anger will not "drive me away," or "blow me away," or "destroy either one of us." Then the anger can be redirected to provide a powerful, corrective emotional experience.

When the therapist notices nonverbal anger signals or cues, it is appropriate to ask clients about their feelings. For example, "Are you feeling angry?" or "You look upset. Are you?" This may be the first time in their lives that someone has responded to them openly, honestly, and appropriately. Having their feelings validated can have a significant and positive healing effect.

The Desire to Please

Because many of these patients were cast in the role of caretaker in their families, some learned to please others in order to be loved. This often resulted in their being unable to identify their own needs, much less fulfill them. They may not be capable of asking the therapist for what they want or sharing what might be bothering them.

These patients' low self-esteem and devalued self-concept force them, quite frequently, to adopt submissive attitudes in order to be accepted and loved. At times, this strong need to be valued place them in fragile and vulnerable situation when they display these loving needs, thereby creating situations where they can be exploited again.

Many patients learned to use their caretaking skills as a buffer to control and regulate the degree of closeness or distance in their interpersonal relationships. The relationship with the therapist is no exception. Some survivors use a pursuer–distancer dance to avoid and control the risk of being intimate with others and, consequently, to avoid the unconscious expectations of being abandoned or rejected. This can be a confusing and seemingly non-functional dance for the therapist. Nonetheless, it is desirable, especially initially, to follow their lead, move to their rhythm, and learn their maladaptive steps and patterns in order, slowly, to proceed to change and modify their dysfunctional behavior.

Movement into a more functional, harmonious, and intimate dance should be choreographed slowly and carefully because some patients feel overwhelmed by any change by the therapist, and undeserving of the healthier relationship. Caring and awareness of this process are essential to help the patients develop a more flexible, authentic, spontaneous, and balanced view of themselves and their world.

Understanding Sexually Stylized Behaviors

Adult survivors will frequently interact with their therapists in habitual interpersonal behavior patterns. Especially for patients who were sexually abused, these may include the learned response to relate in a sexualized style if the clinician is of the same sex as was the sexual offender.

Some patients do not distinguish sex from more generalized attention or affection, so they may be inappropriately seductive within the therapeutic setting. They may display eroticized or flirtatious ways or dress provocatively. Usually these patients are not seeking sex; they are simply interacting in the only way they know.

Courtois and Sprei (1988) wrote that the adult survivor may view being sexual as a way of expressing affection, of gaining a sense of control that reinforces her belief that anyone who cares about her must want to be sexual, or as a way of giving the only worthwhile thing she believes she has to offer. They further suggested that sexually stylized behaviors may be a way of expressing self-hatred or a way to prove the therapist's venality.

The clinician must set appropriate and clear boundaries within the therapeutic relationship. It is never appropriate, for a therapist to have sexual relations with a patient. Not only is such exploitation illegal and unethical, but it would represent another ultimate betrayal and constitute a devastating victimization. The therapist must take responsibility for protecting the patient from any inappropriate or abusive behaviors.

COUNTERTRANSFERENCE

Countertransference is a phenomenon with important ramifications to which the therapist must always be alert. Just as a patient's perceptions can become distorted by transference, the mental health professional also can fall victim to his or her own reaction to the patient's material.

Currently, there are two different ways of viewing countertransference. These are the so-called narrow definition and the broad definition. The former refers to the idiosyncratic, individualized reaction of the therapist/analyst, intimately connected to an internalized conflict or neurotic problem that interferes with his keeping a neutral therapeutic position, therefore allowing a contamination of the therapeutic process by his own unresolved neurotic conflict and rendering the therapy ineffective. The broad definition of countertransference simply means any emotional reaction on the part of the analyst/therapist to the patient's material whether or not it connects with the therapist's own conflict.

As previously mentioned, the therapist's own reaction to the patient's problem can be a valuable tool in understanding the patient's psychology and allow the therapist to empathize with the patient's experience. The feelings generated – if they are defined and analyzed – can be used to uncover information about the therapist's mental processes and unresolved intrapsychic and interpersonal conflicts, provided the clinician has participated in a process that allows him or her access to such conflicts. These feelings can provide clinicians with special insights and information that are helpful to the psychotherapeutic process in general, and to the patient–therapist relationship in particular. To distinguish between the therapist's actual feelings and those being projected by the patient onto the therapist is essential.

This vignette illustrates the therapeutic use of countertransference:

> The patient was a successful middle-aged professional woman who was subjected to serious emotional abuse and neglect by an alcoholic mother and a passive father figure. The patient had been in therapy for approximately two years. In the midst of a neurotic transference reaction, she brought up a dream in which the predominant theme was about a co-worker violating her "turf" and images of "sharks with teeth ripping her apart." The patient had been struggling in previous sessions with homosexual fears and the feeling that she could not hide

anything from the therapist, feeling a pressure to talk about all her inner feelings and becoming very vulnerable during the session. The patient had always suspected sexual molestation by the mother during one of her frequent episodes of alcoholic intoxication.

The therapist's initial reaction was a need and urge to know more about the patient's secrets, her homosexual fears, and the kinds of things she could no longer hide from the therapist. Becoming aware of these feelings, so strong in this particular session, allowed him to understand that if he were to inquire directly and exhibit curiosity about her sexual secrets and fears, it would be tantamount to a recapitulation of the violation of her turf, as suggested in the dream. The therapist's awareness of a countertransference reaction and his attempts to understand the context of the patient's past and the nature of the transference allowed him to make therapeutic use of the patient's reaction, first, by giving the patient more time to metabolize the material and come up with her own interpretation of her feelings, and second, by avoiding the role of violator of her boundaries.

Briere (1989) points out that the therapist is entering into an intense relationship with an interpersonally dysfunctional individual whose issues may bring forth unresolved aspects of the clinician's early life that may bias the therapist's behaviors, "despite his or her training and professional demeanor" (p. 73). He believes the "two major sources of the therapist's countertransference to abuse-focused psychotherapy are the therapist's own childhood experience of abuse, maltreatment, or neglect, and issues related to therapist gender" (p. 74).

It is most important that the clinicians be aware that countertransference is an ever-present phenomenon and, at the same time, be in touch with and in control of these feelings in order to employ them on the patient's behalf. Therapists who lack this awareness may unconsciously act out these feelings—with the potentially tragic result of a secondary injury to their patients.

Specialized Information and Training

It is the exception rather that the rule that mental health professionals have received adequate professional education and training related to the treatment of adult survivors of childhood abuse and their specific issues. It is widely believed that much misinformation and misunderstanding exists among mental health professionals about issues of emotional, physical, and sexual abuse; at times, myths and taboos, rather than the psychological needs of the patient, predominate and guide the mind of the treater. Other times misapplied theoretical frameworks lead to a neglect of the intrafamilial forces that have contributed to the patient's traumatic experience. More education and exposure of the therapist-in-training to this community problem is needed to adequately address the needs of all the parties involved in this modern epidemic.

Psychotherapy with these patients effectively requires personal preparation. The authors highly recommend that therapists planning to treat adult survivors have completed (or be in the process of completing) their own personal psychoanalysis or psychotherapy and obtain peer or clinical consultation or supervision, participate in a therapists' support group, or engage in other forms of adjunctive, insightful, personal growth-oriented therapy and/or training.

Adult survivor patients are well known for the intensity of the countertransference they evoke in their therapists. Briere (1989) states that counselors "who are still at odds with their abuse, who use denial, dissociation, or splitting to deal with abuse-related dysphoria, are likely to discover that working with other people's victimization issues restimulates their own. This restimulation, in turn, usually increases problems . . . such as PTSD symptoms and over- or under-investment in the client" (p. 74).

In treating the adult survivor of childhood abuse, psychotherapists may experience feelings of empathy, frustration, guilt, rejection, anger, impatience, anxiety, fear, sadness, respect, love, and/or pain. The very important task of therapists is to sort out these emotional reactions and to understand which are part of their own unresolved past issues, which are patient transferential issues, and which are currently being induced by the patient. There is nothing inherently troublesome about the feelings, negative or positive, as long as therapists appropriately identify and deal with the feelings and their source in a manner that advances their patients' progress in treatment.

Clinicians treating adult survivors typically manifest several countertransference reactions. Many therapists find that they experience feelings of pain on hearing adult survivors whose abusive histories mirror their own. The discomfort can lead them to adopt defenses similar to those used by their patients: minimization, denial, projection, rationalization, intellectualization, repression, avoidance, suppression, and/or dissociation.

Some therapists engage in their own denial and avoidance when it comes to treating adult survivors of childhood abuse. They may fail to explore their patients' horrific and disturbing experiences, histories, and feelings. But clinicians must be willing to deal directly with this material. They must also be able to accept calmly the feelings and revelations expressed by patients, and convey that they are willing to hear them. Treaters will neither avoid nor allow patients to avoid dealing with past trauma.

Therapists may unduly minimize some of a patient's abuse experiences by trying to universalize them with statements such as "Everyone is a victim." Other therapists who feel uncomfortable change the subject, encourage the patient "not to think about it," imply that it was "only a dream," or exhort the patient to "pick up the pieces and get on with your life." These responses typically reinforce the patient's feelings of isolation, shame, anger, betrayal, powerlessness, and despair.

Some therapists also may find that they are stimulated by or attracted to the adult survivor's experiences, especially those of victims of sexual abuse. This may be demonstrated by an extreme interest in details of the abuse without appropriate focus on other issues and conflicts as well. Such exploitation can result in the patient feeling revictimized by the therapist.

Any mental health professional who is overly intrusive of patients' boundaries is thereby reenacting the violation of those boundaries, indicating the therapist's own need of professional counseling.

Other psychotherapists react by viewing the patient as damaged goods. This may be manifested in the therapist's tendencies to perceive these victims as overly fragile, helpless, overly special, or powerless. Failing to see their strengths, the therapist overfunctions for them. This only reinforces such patients' sense of dependence, invalidating in turn their sense of autonomy, self-esteem, and self-determination. Peer consultation may enable the therapist to recognize unrealistic feelings of omnipotence and to see how that taps into a personal need to rescue a patient.

Clinicians should fully explore their reactions in working with this patient population as valuable inner clues and signals. The reactions can either be used appropriately to facilitate personal growth or inappropriately to hinder patients' recovery. Atypical feelings of anger, detachment, frustration, helplessness, or any other of the innumerable emotional states should be assessed for their source. Discussions with colleagues about countertransference reactions occurring in the therapeutic process can help clinicians regain the necessary professional distance for continued efficacious treatment.

Since childhood abuse constitutes a highly loaded and multi-dimensional problem, it can arouse feelings of pain for both the patient and the clinician. However, with the therapist's under-

standing of the intricate ebb-and-flow process, the helping relationship can be a meaningful experience for both. The therapist's
affirming and attentive manner to a patient's disclosures of childhood emotional, physical, and/or sexual abuse is necessary to heal
the client's toxic wounds. Together, they can struggle along the
arduous journey to overcome the scars of the past in order to
mobilize and enhance the patient's capacity for a more self-fulfilling,
enriching, and healthy life.

4

The Therapeutic Process

Adult survivors of childhood abuse or trauma vary in both their motivation and capacity as well as their opportunity for psychotherapy. It is vital to be attuned to the multidetermined factors and interdependent variables that affect and influence this dynamic process. Given each individual's idiosyncratic way of manifesting unique but at the same time typical sequelae of abuse, the amount of time each patient spends in each phase is determined by his or her multiplex aspects. Further, the phases of treatment are not clearly distinct at times.

Careful attention and gauging of survivor needs may be a challenging task, since often other (at times unrelated) issues must be handled concurrently. Proper pacing of patient's material, along with well-timed interventions, are critical and invaluable throughout the entire course of therapy.

It is important that the therapist have a frame of reference regarding the three phases of treatment. These are presented below as suggested guidelines, not formulas, to assist the clinician in the continuing assessment, planning, and implementation of appropriate treatment interventions.

INITIAL PHASE OF TREATMENT

Establishing A Meaningful Therapeutic Relationship

Following the completion of the evaluative period as outlined in a previous chapter, the therapist is now in a position to initiate the therapy process per se. It must be kept in mind that there are always overlaps between the evaluation/diagnostic process proper and the initial therapeutic phase since therapeutic elements such as initial bonding, transference reactions, and so on, that the therapist can capitalize on at a later time could very well be operating from the first contact with the patient. Having a clear and detailed view of the patient's biopsychosocial and cultural matrix and assessing how well the patient develops an alliance on evaluation gives the therapist an advantage in terms of guiding the intervention.

The therapist's empathic attitude is an important element throughout the process. A show of authentic interest in the patient and his or her problems should be complemented by a consistent, congruent, and reliable therapeutic atmosphere. Genuine concern in an open, honest climate should permeate the session; that may be the first time the survivor has experienced such a trustworthy relationship.

At the same time a therapeutic environment is being fostered, the clinician must also evince a predictable, safe, and nonjudgmental attitude. Additionally, the therapist needs to maintain clear boundaries and respect for the patient's individuality to facilitate the expression of thoughts and feelings without fear of retaliation. Patients may initially have difficulty sharing their pain, and only the therapist's sensitivity, empathic attunement, and encouragement will alleviate this fear, which at times will pervade the treatment process. An element of hope and an optimism about patients' healing and capacity for growth are extremely important, since many survivors feel a sense of hopelessness about their plight.

Any artificial, incongruent, or patronizing behavior on the part of the therapist has no place in psychotherapy. The therapist should be aware that many of these patients will be hypervigilant to such behavior and will challenge and retest it. The patients' need for closeness and the fear generated by realizing an attachment to the therapist, coupled with the past traumatic experience(s), will account for that hypervigilant, suspicious behavior manifested by these patients, especially during the initial phase of treatment.

At times, patients will exhibit symptomatology that may initially require the introduction of parameters to contain the open expression of aggressive behavior toward the self or others, such as pharmacological treatment or even hospitalization to stabilize the patient and provide a safe, secure environment. Not uncommonly, patients have a dual diagnosis, making it necessary to address issues that may or may not be related to the original traumatic experience. The uppermost priority in the initial phase of treatment is to prevent any self-inflicted harm, and the therapist's task is to actively inquire about such tendencies openly and empathically.

Suicidal behavior, self-mutilation, outbursts of self-destructive rage, and homicidal ideation can present either as separate diagnostic entities or as symptoms disguising the core trauma(s). Either way the priority is prevention or containment of that type of behavior by intervening early and decisively. The therapist should clarify for the patient how such a crisis will be handled and must also make herself available in a consistent way within reasonable and previously mutually agreed-upon parameters.

Patients suffering severe character pathology, such as borderline personality disorder, will present a greater challenge and will require more complex interventions than patients whose borderline-type presentation reflects a way of coping with trauma but who basically have a personality organized at a higher level. Again, a good pre-therapy assessment is extremely vital and valuable under these circumstances.

Patients' Salient Issues

Lack of empowerment, dysfunctional and survival coping mechanisms, lack of trust, and lack of belief in self—for patients with a history of abuse, these are the most typical and salient issues. As a matter of fact, these issues have almost always been identified in the initial period of treatment of our patient population. Of course, there are other clearly recognizable problems that will acquire different degrees of importance as the therapy process unfolds.

Lack of empowerment is usually the pivotal issue for survivors in this phase of treatment. The therapist must encourage and support the patient's developing a sense of autonomy. Just the fact that he has decided to seek psychotherapy for his problem is a step toward healing and empowerment. The therapist should value the patient's attempt at self-growth and encourage him to set goals for treatment. The patient's desire, courage, and motivation to change need to be validated. He needs to be allowed to make appropriate choices that clearly reflect his own sociocultural background. If the therapist keeps an open mind and maintains a degree of neutrality, sooner or later the patient will regain a feeling of self-confidence and of being capable to make his own decisions. Any evidence of constructive change or clear progress in his ability to communicate, express feelings, or demonstrate changes in attitudes and behaviors should be supported by the therapist.

Engaging patients in an active role, rather than having them simply be passive recipients of advice or guidelines, allows them to regain control of their lives while letting go of helplessness. Questions such as "What has worked for you before?" "What were the greatest barriers in your path?" "How did you overcome them?" "What did you discover about yourself during that situation?" "What are your alternatives in this situation?" can set in motion a process that will encourage patients to use their potential.

Adult survivors begin the treatment process armed with dysfunctional coping mechanisms. Patients who have suffered a history of trauma can make use of practically any kind of defense mechanism that has been described in the psychiatric literature. How the individual actually coped with the traumatic event probably depends on factors such as how advanced in psychological development the victim was; a combination of age at onset and duration, frequency, and intensity of the abuse; how severe or fragmenting the trauma(s) were; the coexistence of other pathological processes; the biological constitution and/or the emotional resiliency of the individual; the type(s) of trauma(s); the relationship of the perpetrator(s) to the victim; the use or absence of force; and the environmental response to the disclosure.

Leaving aside the coexistence of other pathological processes or comorbidity and postulating the existence of a posttraumatic adaptation in a more classical presentation, the therapist's task is primarily to reframe the patient's present behavior as adaptive responses or accommodations to the abuse or trauma. Thus the patient's way of coping could be viewed as survival tools, though no longer adaptive. Helping the patient view her behavior from that angle and being able to understand and connect the current behavior to the past abuse is the beginning of the change toward more adaptive behavior. Confronting her with her dysfunctional way of coping is nonproductive and could easily be interpreted by the patient as criticism.

The therapist's view of the patient's defenses as normal reactions to an abnormal event and efforts to de-pathologize the behavior will have a normalizing effect and be reassuring to the patient, and that in itself may lead to a decrease in dysfunctional ways of coping. Clarification and interpretation can also be very helpful.

Therapists must avoid responding with shock or surprise to the adult survivor's disclosures or descriptions of how they have dealt with the abuse. Patients may have coped with the trauma in regressed or dysfunctional ways, in which the use of primitive mechanisms such as splitting, projection, projective identification, primitive denial, and idealization may have predominated. Other patients would have used dissociation, rationalization, repression, or somatization. Each individual's ways of coping will translate into symptoms. The process of uncovering, disclosing, and discharging emotions coupled with the therapist's empathy and support will surely pave the way for the use of new functional behavior with a diminution of the old symptomatology. Consequently, issues of helplessness, shame, guilt, unlovability, fears of abandonment, anxieties, and depression will come to the fore as the so-called defense begins to disappear. Some survivors who "looked good" on first meeting will look and feel worse.

Lack of trust is the third critical issue of the beginning phase of treatment for survivors. Fostering an atmosphere of open, honest disclosure may be a difficult task; only through the therapist's patience, consistency, and trustworthy behavior will the patient change his understandable mistrust of the world. Relationship building is a gradual process with these patients.

The desire and need to disclose can be equal only to the fear of punishment. The two grew together and became inseparable aspects of the patient's pain and helplessness. Reliability and congruency are the main ingredients of a therapeutic relationship leading to an increased development of trust. Maintaining clear boundaries of the therapeutic alliance and accepting one's limitations are also essential to the healing process.

The last salient issue of this first phase of treatment of the adult survivor is the lack of belief in self. Because most patients are guilt-ridden and were in many ways made to believe that they were responsible for what happened to them, they suffer from a lack of trust in themselves manifested by a lack of self-confidence and a lack of assertiveness, which reflects low self-esteem and a devalued self-image. With patients who are psychologically ready, the therapist can begin gradually to identify and label abusive behavior on the part of the perpetrators as well as holding them accountable for it. This reframing of the self-blame cognitive distortion should result in a gradual decrease of guilt. Reframing statements may prove helpful, for example, "You are not responsible for the offender's behavior"; "Something wrong did happen to you, but it wasn't your fault"; "You were just a helpless child at the time"; "Abuse is something that happened to you; it's not who you are." One caveat: with a decrease in the self-blame underlying feelings of helplessness and/or powerlessness, patients may need the help of the therapist to contain and modulate some of the intensity of those feelings.

It is desirable for the therapist to begin to validate any movement toward assertive behavior and accept the patient's thoughts and feelings as real and important. An attitude of acceptance will increase the patient's self-reliance and self-trust. The therapist can verbalize that the patient's fears are justified under the circumstances. Further, elaborating on the variety of feelings the patient may have about the past experiences introduces a powerful element of reality that leads to a re-experience of anger, which now can be redirected to mobilize the patient's potentiality, aided by the empathy of the clinician.

Risks in the Initial Phase of Treatment

In the beginning phase of treatment, many factors contributing to the therapy process can interfere with the treatment and will not be elaborated on here. However, those connected with the treatment process that could result in a premature termination deserve mention and can be divided in two different categories: those contributed by the patient, and those contributed by the therapist.

Some patients leave therapy prematurely out of a sense of system relief, thinking treatment is no longer needed. Other patients develop a negative therapeutic reaction generated by any number of psychological factors, including guilt, a sense of not deserving to feel better, a perceived empathic failure, a negative transference reaction, or an uncontrollable fear of being revictimized.

The therapist, in turn, may consciously or unconsciously interact in such a way that will convey to the patient that she is not believable, or he may minimize the patient's disclosure by being distant or too involved, by being judgmental, by violating the patient's boundaries, or by not being empathic. Surely, any one of these could lead to a re-victimization of the patient.

MIDDLE OR CORE PHASE OF TREATMENT

There are no clear-cut boundaries between the initial and middle phases of treatment. There is also overlap of the different phases of treatment, though specific problem areas will unfold as the process of therapy continues. They will be colored by the patient's individual way of working, the core defenses, and resistance.

As the therapeutic alliance is consolidated and layers of resistance are penetrated, the treater will be able to conceptualize the process in different phases.

Naturally, the therapist's empathic position should be maintained throughout the therapeutic process, as well as his "suspended attention" that will allow for a check of his own reaction to the patient's material as well as scrutiny of the patient's transference reaction and the overall intersubjective field.

The treater should view the therapy process as an opportunity to continuously reassess the patient's progress, how the process itself is unfolding, what impact the treatment is having on both the patient's level of functioning and relationships with the outside world.

Perhaps the single most important aspect of the therapeutic process during its middle phase is the working through of the patient's internalized conflict.

Working Through

Even though ill defined and interpreted in different ways in the psychoanalytic literature, working through is widely accepted as an intrapsychic process by which the patient is able to correct long-standing misperception and chronic distortions of her own inner reality.

Working through involves a "recognition and assimilation of newly learned truths, an alteration of balance among the defenses, neutralization of resistance, formation of new identifications and reconstruction of the Ego Ideal" (Hinsie and Campbell 1974, p. 814).

The working through of the patient's traumatic event is facilitated by, and to a large extent reflects, the arduous and painful vicissitudes of the overall therapeutic process. It is only by virtue of consistent, empathic interaction that the patient begins to internalize a trusting, benign figure of the therapist that will later translate into long-lasting changes. Working through is a realignment of internal objects through introjection of and identification with the therapist that frequently leads to structural changes and a decrease in the inter- and intrasystemic conflict(s) generated by past abuse. For example, internalizing the nonjudgmental, nonpunitive, trustworthy figure of the therapist could foster a less rigid, less guilt-provoking superego. That in itself would allow energy previously spent in compromise formation to be put to use in the process of adjusting and adapting to a new reality. Identifying with the analyst (or therapist) is the basis for expanding and reconstructing the ego ideal, which stimulates future goal attainment and is the source of realistic self-esteem (Karush 1967).

Tasks of the Therapist

Insight-producing clarifications and interpretations, along with other supportive interventions such as reframing, will help the patient to see the distortions in the way he or she perceives reality. The patient's affective response on recalling memories of the abuse will gradually decrease in intensity, creating a positive, self-feeding cycle (as illustrated in Figure 4–1) in which the decrease in the distortion will increase the patient's capacity for objective self-perception, which in turn will decrease self-blame and increase self-esteem.

Another goal of therapy during the core phase of treatment is

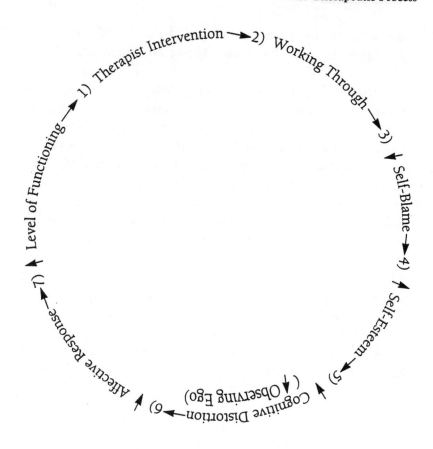

Figure 4-1. Self-feeding positive cycle

the positive resolution of the trauma. To achieve this end, the therapist needs to maintain a safe environment to enable the patient to work realistically through the traumatic events that distort his or her psychological world.

At the most positive level the patient will be able to put the trauma in an appropriate perspective by reliving the abuse, shedding related dysfunctional defenses while openly experiencing, resolving, and integrating the once-hidden feelings and memories. Simultaneously, the therapist's task is to reappraise concomitant cognitively distorted schemas, making a significant advance toward resolution of the trauma. Also, the patient must come to terms with the realization that she was the victim and not accountable for the abuse. By being able to work through and place the trauma in the past, the patient will not be influenced by or reexperience it in the present. This contributes to a mastery of the trauma.

Additional tasks of the therapist during this process are to encourage cognitive reappraisals, to assist the patient to modulate the painful affect, to help mobilize and increase the patient's capacity for self-soothing and self-calming, and to monitor the patient's reactions and behaviors related to reconstruction of the trauma process.

To help the patient pace or "dose" traumatic material is another important task of the therapist. Working through the abuse will involve moving back and forth from exploration to consolidation. In other words, the therapist assists the patient in moving to and through the traumatic material and then away from it, thereby gaining the growth-producing benefits that enable the patient to continue to deal with additional traumatic material. Typically, this process is both gradual and laborious; the goal is to enable the patient to progress from the role of victim to survivor to thriver.

Desexualization of the Abuse

With sexual abuse in particular, it is important to help the patients realize that the incident was a violent abuse of power, that it was not their fault, and that they have the right to express their anger in a guilt-free, nonjudgmental atmosphere. It is very reassuring for patients to realize there was nothing sexual about the abuse (in the case of rape, molestation, or incest), but rather that it was a violation of boundaries, a traumatic event over which they had no control whatsoever and for which they were not responsible, though they may have been led to believe so. This apparently simple intervention, ego-supportive in nature, sometimes is the turning point that sets in motion the positive, self-feeding psychological cycle described earlier, in which a correction of the cognitive distortions in the context of a proper therapeutic atmosphere leads to long-lasting psychological changes.

There are supportive interventions that have proven to be valuable particularly in the initial phase of treatment that facilitate the development of a working relationship. Among them are the following:

1. Validate and encourage autonomous action consistently.
2. Validate realistic feelings and adaptive behaviors.
3. Affirm patient's realistic strengths.
4. Encourage patient's attempts at healthy risk taking so long as there is a reasonable hope of success.
5. Engage in psychoeducational intervention about sexuality and normal physiological sexual responses as well as other life-enhancing topics by encouraging the use of audio- and video-tapes, books, and so on, with patients who have a specific sexual abuse history.
6. Encourage the patient to join adjunctive therapy groups to reduce his or her sense of isolation and invisibility.

Impact of Therapy on Ego Functions

During this middle or core phase, it will be evident how the process of treatment is positively influencing the patient's level of functioning as measured by his ego capacities. The process of working-through, as previously described, with all of its ramifications, coupled with a realignment of the patient's internalized world of objects catalyzed by internalization of the therapist, will lead to structural changes. Ego growth can be measured by the patient's improved capacity to test reality in a more appropriate and objective way; the patient should be able to better tolerate situations of stress and anxiety and to exercise an increased control of impulses, areas that are commonly troublesome for this patient population.

The correction of the patient's distortion implies a more benign, modified superego more realistic in its demands of a beleaguered ego, thus decreasing intersystemic tension evident in a decrease of self-blame, unrealistic guilt, and the adoption of a more flexible standard of behavior.

Judgment, the capacity to chose a sensible alternative or to make a decision that best fits an individual's needs, will also improve as treatment continues.

Quality of Object Relationships

We have established how crucial the figure of the therapist and the internalization of that figure is to the therapeutic process. The changes in the patient's negatively charged self and object representation to a positively invested self-object representation and further integration and neutralization of contradictory ego states are fundamental. These changes will powerfully influence structural changes that will allow for better regulation of affect and impulse. A better object representation improves interpersonal relationships and permits the patient to enter a positive, self-feeding cycle in which he or she can both give to others and receive from others, the latter leading to an increase in both self-esteem and positive object representation, completing the cycle.

Defensive Operations

Automatic patterns of coping will also be affected by the growth of the mental structure and the decrease of intra- and intersystemic conflicts. Being able to contain and modulate feelings appropriately could reflect a basic change from primitive, dysfunctional defensive operations to a higher, healthier, and more adaptive way of coping.

A need to project out blame to alleviate feelings of guilt, decrease inner tension, contaminating and distorting reality in the process, may be the only psychological alternative for some traumatized patients. Introjection of, and further identification with, the rejecting or abusive object can be considered another line of defense, however primitive and dysfunctional that line may be. Introjection is a more primitive form of internalization, an incomplete metabolism of the object, which remains unintegrated with the self but still has power to control the patient's behavior. At times, introjection and projection go hand in hand. The introjected object or part-object is always contaminated by projection, so that the introject, whether good or bad, is a combination of real object plus the positive or negative aspects projected on the object.

Further metabolism of the introject and integration with the self leads to "identification units," or building blocks in which the self gradually takes in the attributes of the objects. This results in the so-called identification with the aggressor mechanism described by A. Freud (1936), which explains why survivors of abuse are at times abusers themselves. However, not all abused children become abusers as adults. In fact, only 25 to 30 percent of abused children maltreat their offspring. That means that the majority of survivors do not either abuse their own children or identify with a victim role (Okula 1987). In certain circumstances they become the victimizer and in the process deny their past helplessness to the authority, the powerful figure, the aggressor. As structural changes begin to take hold and patients begin to use higher-level defenses, inner tension decreases and distortions are corrected; sublimatory channels develop, along with a better capacity to verbalize feelings appropriately. The changes in the defensive operation are byproducts of the restructuring taking place under the influence of changing object relationships. The same applies to other ego functions, as the therapeutic process promotes further ego growth.

Risks of the Middle Phase of Treatment

The risks involved in this treatment phase are similar to those at the beginning of treatment, with some exceptions.

Throughout treatment there is always a risk of the patient interrupting the process, whether because of negative transference, insurmountable resistance, a flight into health, a decrease in motivation, or numerous other factors.

At times, the patient lacks ego resources, which limits the therapy to less ambitious goals. External events (unavoidable moves, changes in life situation, and so on) could also interrupt the process, forcing an early termination phase.

TERMINATION PHASE OF TREATMENT

As the process of working-through promotes a resolution of the patient's conflicts and he or she experiences a new internal reality, the patient begins to indicate readiness to terminate treatment.

Usually the patient initiates the process of discussing the end of the therapy. Clearly, the patient is the one separating from the therapist, whose role at this point is to participate in a mutual assessment of what has been achieved in a realistic way and to facilitate, if appropriate, the patient's attempt at autonomous functioning.

For some patients the termination phase is as important, and at times more important, than the working-through phase. Issues of abandonment, perceived rejection, separation anxiety, and related conflicts are frequently reactivated during this phase. The literature reports widely that during the termination process issues that brought the patient into therapy are often reactivated, but now the patient is able to use insight to formulate his or her own interpretation and to try out new independence.

Tasks of the Therapist

The therapist's task during this final phase of treatment are to assess the patient's readiness for termination, to identify the goals achieved by the patient and the patient's behavioral changes, and to facilitate the separation.

Criteria for Termination

Achievement of Treatment Goals

Patients should be encouraged to recount their experience, since successful goals should be congruent with changes in both behavior and symptomotolgy. The affective component in patients' verbalization of their achievement should also be congruent. Patients frequently experience a sense of mastery of the trauma or internalized conflict(s) and demonstrate the courage to move on to a more autonomous life, often expressing pleasure in their achievements and interpersonal relationships.

As patients review the therapeutic process, there should be evidence of a decrease in the intensity of the affect previously attached to the now-resolved trauma or conflict. A decrease of old fears, guilt, anxiety, and other feelings should be evident as the patient enters the final phase of treatment.

Ambivalence about Termination

Patients frequently enter this final phase of treatment with marked ambivalence and doubts about whether they are ready to be on their own. This situation resembles what Mahler and colleagues (1975) describe as a "practicing period," a subphase of the separation–individuation process. Patients will begin to test the water and to give signals and clues about their readiness to begin separation from the therapist.

They will expect validation of their experienced success from the therapist, always with a mixture of anxiety and fear, but also with a sense of accomplishment and gratification.

Transference

Whether the tranferential issues have been the exclusive focus of the therapist's intervention, as is frequently the case with higher-functioning patients in expressive psychoanalytically oriented therapy or psychoanalysis, or whether the therapist skillfully neglected to use tranferential material during the therapeutic process, transference is always present as a universal phenomenon. During the termination process it is quite possible to observe, in patients previously functioning at a lower level, an increased capacity to work on this type of material. Some patients become curious to learn more about themselves once their traumatic events have been worked-through. At times, a switch to a different, more analytically oriented process is indicated to improve the patient's desire for self-realization via indepth examination.

Consolidation of Ego Growth

The therapeutic process is not a linear one; it may be best described as a circular process in which improvements in psychic functioning (ego, self, superego) stimulate changes in behavior forming a self-feeding cycle.

Clinically it is evident that an improvement in the quality of a patient's object relationship (an ego function) will translate into better interpersonal relationships and an improved observing-ego capacity. Better awareness of one's contribution to reality enables the individual to tolerate and contain frustration and to exercise better control over behavior and impulses.

Thus, during the termination phase there should be a final consolidation of the growth of the ego function compromised by trauma. Secondary pathological symptoms and impaired functioning should decrease as well.

In most cases, perhaps with the questionable exception of the very high functioning trauma patient, there would be clinical evidence of structural deficits either at the ego or superego level. These deficits may have affected only discrete areas of the ego or superego, or they may have been pervasive, affecting ego functioning at all levels. At any rate, the termination phase should highlight the psychological healing and growth that has taken place. All changes resulting from therapeutic interactions previously elaborated should permit the treater to clearly identify the behavioral signs that indicate the patient's higher level of functioning, such as:

1. Developing a wide repertoire of resources, new functional skills, and behaviors to deal effectively with problems in a mature and independent manner. These skills may be evidenced by: feelings of empowerment and assertiveness; an ability to differentiate boundaries; a capacity for limit setting; an increased capacity for self-examination and self-acceptance; an increased capacity for introspection; a solid sense of mastery over his life.

2. Developing the ability to identify needs and wants and to satisfy them (as well as needs of others, when appropriate) in a safe, functional way.

3. Developing a capacity for trust of self and others.

4. Being able to identify and express appropriately a wide spectrum of feelings.

5. Developing coping skills, as reflected in a capacity to be alone, to self-soothe, and to eliminate self-blame for the abuse. The

patient is able to reassign responsibility where it belongs and to forgive himself.

6. Increasing self-esteem, which will also contribute to feelings of being lovable and valuable. Being able to see both his "good" and "bad" aspects allows the patient to assess his internal world more realistically.

7. Developing and consolidating self-identity, which aids in setting clearer and more realistic goals.

8. Developing a capacity to enjoy and tolerate intimacy (including sexual relationships) without feeling threatened, and without fearing engulfment and desintegration. This capacity is usually manifested by feelings of mutuality, respect, trust, authenticity, acceptance, and empathy.

All of the above, combined with the elimination of symptoms and lack of acting out of the abuse or needing to re-create the trauma, are the final indications of its resolution. At times, the partial achievement alone of these goals translates into dramatic improvement in the patient's life and behavior. Ideally, the therapist should see an overall improvement in the way the patient relates to himself and a better quality of interaction with others. The patient has transformed distorted schemata into realistic ones, accommodated to a different reality, forgiven him- or herself, and entered a new, higher level of functioning.

5

Psychodynamic Treatment Strategies

PSYCHOANALYTIC CONTRIBUTIONS

As early as 1890 Freud ascribed the etiology of neurotic disorders to past traumatic events and thought that an effective cure could be achieved by abreaction and the working-through of the traumatic event once the memory of the trauma was recovered. Freud's ideas constantly changed and evolved from topographic theory to a structural conceptualization of the mental apparatus. The traumatic theory of neurosis lost ground to conflicts generated by intersystemic (or intrasystemic) tension. However, in *Inhibitions, Symptoms and Anxiety* (1926) Freud placed renewed emphasis on the notion of trauma as the cause of the neurosis, though now embedded in the defensive operation of the ego. The process could be explained as follows.

Where the ego was overwhelmed previously by the traumatic event, that is, neglect, or emotional, physical, or sexual abuse, the ego develops a capacity to release a signal of anxiety to avoid being overwhelmed again; the danger is now being generated from inside in anticipation of the painful experience. Repressed mechanisms could cause it to take the form of fear of unknown origin. In other words, the ego is being attacked from inside, thus forcing a specific set of defensive operations that varies from individual to individual. These defensive operations translate into symptomatic behavior. As illustrated in chapter 2, the traumatic event can create a fragmentation and leave long-lasting effects on the overall post-trauma organization of the victim's personality. Factors such as level of ego growth at time of the trauma and the impact on other developmental currents can play an important role in the specific symptoms a patient will exhibit.

The psychoanalytic definition of trauma is pertinent. In psychoanalytic language, a trauma is "an event in the subject's life defined by its intensity, by the subject's incapacity to respond adequately to it, and by the upheaval and long-lasting effects that it brings about in the psychic organization. In economic terms, the trauma is characterized by an influx of excitation that is excessive by the standards of the subject's tolerance and capacity to master such excitations and work them out psychically" (Laplanche and Pontalis 1973, p. 465).

Contemporary psychoanalysis has evolved from the rigid, drive-oriented conceptualization of the etiology of neurotic disorders to a more inclusive body of knowledge that incorporates other models such as Mahler's ideas about the separation–individuation process, Kohut's self-psychological approach, and a further elaboration and reconceptualization of Melanie Klein's ideas of the internalization of object relationships.

As previously mentioned, Freud (1905a) first believed that real trauma was the etiology of hysteria. Freud's abandonment of the so-called seduction theory, for reasons that are historically unclear, led him to elaborate a theory based on the role of sexual fantasies as the cause of neurotic disorder. Based on this "new" conceptualization, Freud considered the *fantasy* of the seduction, which amounted to a child's imagined sexual abuse by an adult having the same impact as a real traumatic event, as the actual etiology of the neurotic disorders.

The controversy surrounding this issue (fantasy versus real trauma) still haunts the psychoanalytic field. For some, Freud's shift contributed to a neglect of real events in the life of the individual that might have played a crucial role in the formation of character and subsequent neurotic development and symptom formation.

In working with patients with an identifiable history of physical, emotional, or sexual abuse, the analyst (therapist) should take the patient's memories of the traumatic event at face value, as real happenings in the life of the child until proven otherwise; at the very least the patient's evoked memories of any traumatic event should not be qualified or judged as the product of an overactive sexual fantasy life of a child with unresolved oedipal conflicts.

There is ample room in the psychoanalytic field to work harmoniously with the two types of patient populations—those who readily identify early, true traumatic events in their lives and those whose neurotic disorder can be traced back to a more complex elaboration and further internalization of sexual fantasies in which the psychoanalytic process has failed to identify a clear-cut, real traumatic event. It is important to maintain a nonjudgmental attitude and let the process uncover the true cause underlying the neurosis.

The psychoanalytic process is the method par excellence that allows the treater to maintain that level of neutrality so long as the analyst is able to avoid ideological rigidity, which can confine the patient to a specific theoretical framework. Theoretical flexibility and open-mindedness are essential components of current psychoanalytic trends and the minimum we should offer patients with suspected or identified history of childhood trauma. The eclectic approach suggested in chapter 2 regarding the evaluation/diagnostic process would be matched only by the same approach to managing the actual analytic/therapeutic work with this patient population.

CONTRIBUTIONS FROM SELF PSYCHOLOGY

In addition to the standard approach (classical or ego psychology-oriented) used in a regular psychoanalytic practice, other currents are effective and have made substantial contributions to work with trauma victims.

A self-psychology approach to understanding victims of trauma tends to bridge or minimize the controversy surrounding the reality-versus-fantasy issue. Ulman and Brothers (1988) argue that "it is neither reality nor fantasy that causes trauma but, rather, that the unconscious meaning of real occurrences causes trauma by shattering central organizing fantasies of self in relation to self objects" (p. 2). They refer to fantasies as having unconscious meanings [widely accepted in the psychoanalytic field], and they add, "If these 'meanings structures' [the unconscious meanings of the fantasies] reflect archaic narcissistic fantasies, they are extremely vulnerable to traumatic shattering and faulty [defensive or compensation] restoration" (p. 2).

This is a very helpful way to begin to understand the impact a traumatic event may have had in a child. It allows us to see the ramifications of the event in terms of how the self may be arrested or delayed in its formation, with clinical implications such as symptom formation, as the fragmented self seeks homeostasis. It also helps us keep an integrated view of how unconscious fantasies (archaic, organizing, narcissistically charged fantasies) play a role vis-à-vis the actual event in the attempts at restoring a sense of wholeness.

The working through of this dynamic (not of the impact of the trauma per se but the further fantasy elaboration and interpretation of the event by the mind of the child) will be the crucial conflict to be resolved. That will be the crux of the psychoanalytic/therapeutic process. This approach automatically removes the controversy of real versus fantasy trauma from the foreground of the treatment or evaluation process.

Kohutian-oriented therapy or analysis has at its core the concept of self and its development. Any factor that interferes with the ability of the self (as an independent, autonomous agency of the mind responsible for "organiz[ing] the meaning of experience") to function or develop is considered a trauma. Therefore, a self psychology-oriented therapeutic or analytic process will aim not only at uncovering the traumatic event (if not readily remembered by the patient) but also at understanding how that central-organizing, underdeveloped self dealt with the event and how the treatment process will aid the healing of the fragmentation and how the therapist's "self-object functions" will help reestablish a sense of self (Kohut 1977).

CONTRIBUTIONS FROM OBJECT RELATIONS THEORY

Most childhood physical, sexual, and emotional abuse takes place in the context of a family dysfunction. In a recent paper Husley and colleagues (1992) report that abused patients almost universally described their families as dysfunctional by interfering with the individual's move toward autonomy and assertiveness; those patients described an authoritarian family where free verbalization of feelings was not allowed. The authors add: "Abused subjects reported that they received no encouragement to participate in social and intellectual activities that foster individualization and the development of autonomous functioning" (p. 448).

Furthermore, their findings support catastrophic consequences in terms of the individual's internalized world of objects. The authors conclude, "It is the embedding of the childhood sexual trauma within such an object relational matrix that appears to be the most significant finding" (p. 448). They add, "This finding supports the contention that the interaction between developmental dynamics and the occurrence of sexual abuse is paramount in determining the final psychopathological outcome of abuse, rather than a casual pathway deriving from the trauma alone" (p. 448).

Clearly, childhood abuse takes place most frequently in the world of object interactions and relationships of the child. The experience of the abuse becomes part of the internalization process and can have a significant impact on the normal processes of introjection, internalization, and identification. The impact of the abuse is measured against the ways in which it interferes with different developmental currents. In the case of the development of object relationships and future quality of the individual's interpersonal and intrapersonal relationships, the impact on the future adult will depend a great deal on how the internalization process was interfered with and how that translated into structural deficits and/or organizational/interstructural (ego, superego, ego ideal, self) tension and conflicts. Kernberg (1976) postulated that there is a direct correlation between the quality of internalized object relationships and the differentiation and solidification of different mental structures.

Since the above is part of a more complex family dysfunction and parental figures or meaningful caretakers are an integral component of the introjected experiences of a child, it follows that the trauma is intimately interconnected with the child's perception of family members and their role in the life of the child. The structural deficits or weaknesses detected in the clinical evaluation of victims of childhood trauma can take the form of different psychiatric syndromes that may disguise the actual trauma. For instance, a patient may present with a symptomatology compatible with a borderline syndrome (both descriptive and structurally) in addition to an identifiable history of childhood abuse. The focus of the treatment should not only be the trauma per se but all the different ramifications it had for the patient's personality dysfunction, its manifestation in the patient's poor quality of object relationship, the dysregulation of affect that often accompanies this type of disorder, among other gross manifestations. Frequently, what is recapitulated in the patient–therapist relationship is the poor quality of parent–child relationship, and that is what commonly colors the transference reactions. Using an object relations approach allows the treater an integrated view of how the abuse affected that developmental current.

Flexibility in working with victims of abuse (whether the abuse was identified prior to initiating treatment or uncovered as part of the psychoanalytic or psychotherapeutic process) allows the clinician to assess the impact of the trauma from different theoretical frames of reference (self psychology, object relations, cognitive or structural analysis) and assures a choice of treatment modality most likely to help the patient.

OTHER CONTRIBUTIONS FROM CLINICAL PSYCHOANALYSIS

Transference-Countertransference in Work with Trauma Patients

The analysis and exploration of transference–countertransference reactions is a crucial aspect of any highly expressive psychotherapy or psychoanalysis. As alluded to in a previous chapter, countertransferential reactions can be used effectively as a tool to enhance and foster the therapeutic process. Countertransference is frequently, though not exclusively, the result and manifestation of projective-identification mechanisms.

A proper handling of this seemingly dysfunctional dyadic situation could dictate the positive outcome of the therapy. Victims of sexual, physical, or emotional abuse may have a distorted perception of themselves accentuated by the buildup of unpleasant feelings generated by the abuse. These patients frequently try to cope with their inner tensions by projecting (transferring) onto others negative introject. They see themselves and their own conflicts in others as if in a mirror. The therapist, therefore, is a prime recipient of these conflicting feelings. At times transference manifests in attempts at molding the therapist into the rejecting, abusive, internalized negative introject. Transference can also force the therapist to play the role of the negative introject, a reaction recognized as countertransference. This reaction is alien to the therapist but can nevertheless exercise control of and interfere with the therapist's feelings and behavior. By being aware of this situation (the intersubjective field) the therapist can gain insight into the patient's conflicts and use that insight to guide the intervention(s). Viewing a patient's transference from such a vantage enhances the therapist's capacity to make more effective interventions. It certainly allows for a more empathic relationship with the patient. For some, empathy is a high-level form of projective identification used for therapeutic purposes.

The transference reactions of adults with identified childhood abuse are frequently very intense and develop rapidly. In classical terms transference is defined as "a process of actualization of unconscious wishes" (Laplanche and Pontalis 1973, p. 455). It is more complex than simply reliving unconscious wishes and infantile longings. Transference reactions very frequently encompass whole object relations units, along with their positive and negative affective components; understanding the transference reaction provides a link to past interactions and relationships between self and objects and/or self and self-objects; they can be projected and attached (transferred) to new relationships in the patient's life such as the developing patient–therapist relationship.

A trauma (here used to mean the self-psychology concept of trauma, as previously described, as it is experienced in the context of a relationship in which the adult perpetrator of the abuse had self-object functions) conceivably will cause more disorganization of the self and will interfere more with the patient's capacity for object relationships than abuse perpetrated by unknown individuals. Ultimately, these factors will color the patient's transference reactions; the therapist's role as self-object for the patient will be fertile ground for development of intense transference reactions, with attendant clinical ramifications.

Silence in the Transference

Silence does not always mean resistance to the analytic or therapeutic work. In fact, at times silence can be a powerful healer. It should be handled like any other piece of psychological material and considered to be multidetermined.

Frequently, when working with trauma patients, one finds that the abused child has been forced by the perpetrator to remain silent because of overt threats of punishment by violence. As the transference evolves and the patient becomes ambivalently attached to the analyst/therapist, the need to contain the details of the abuse, the fear of opening up, of not being accepted or believed, can become a powerful factor that forces the patient to remain silent. The need to remain silent because of fear of retaliation is vividly relived in the therapeutic relationship. To interpret the silence of trauma patients as resistance to treatment is in our view a mistake that could lead to premature termination and further victimization. There are trauma patients whose silence can be traced back to loyalty conflicts, as if breaking the silence were a violation of "loyalty" (a distorted mental schema); other patients may fear being blamed if they open up; still others remain silent as the result of an issue of power/control. Only by keeping in mind the context, and maintaining a flexible and empathic position will the analyst/therapist be able to help the patient eliminate the prohibition against opening up or whatever other factor interferes with full disclosure of the trauma and sharing the experience of abuse.

Pseudosexualization of the Transference

Pseudosexualization of the therapeutic relationship is a common clinical problem in working with sexually abused patients. The treater–patient relationship is not immune to the patient's attempts to master the psychological injury of the trauma by trying in the therapy to duplicate the unfortunate event.

It is difficult to understand why a painful event in the life of an individual would seek to repeat itself. We can ask ourselves what mental agency is responsible for such a tendency, seemingly devoid of any adaptive elements, and what might be the wish fulfillment of such behavior. But the tendency of patients to compulsively repeat the past is an irrefutable fact, a frequently observed clinical phenomenon in the psychoanalytic field.

Freud himself (1920) struggled with this particular issue, at the center of his essay "Beyond the Pleasure Principle," in which he elaborated on the term "repetition compulsion." There is no universal agreement among analysts on the explanation of repetition compulsion. Most analysts would agree, however, that there is an aspect of it related to the attempt of the ego to master the trauma and discharge excessive tension. Patients under the influence of an unconscious need to repeat within or apart from the transference are frequently not aware that an old experience is being repeated. They believe that their feelings and behavior are determined only by current events and circumstances. But some patients who have been emotionally, physically, or sexually abused retain recollection of the traumatic event and are aware of it before treatment starts or may become clearly aware of it in the course of treatment. The tendency to sexualize the relationship should be assessed by the power lens of the clinical microscope and should be differentiated from repressed sexual wishes that are more frequently seen in other types of neurotic disorders. To interpret the sexual fantasies of sexually abused patients as an expression of unconscious wishes generated by the transference reaction may be only partially true in some cases. It is frequently misleading and a disservice to such patients since the pseudosexual behavior of the patient may be preoedipal and/or defensive in nature. Once the patient feels understood by an empathic analyst/therapist and the issue of the trauma is in the process of being resolved, then any other transferential distortion would become apparent and the patient would be more receptive to an interpretation of the neurotic side of his or her perception of the relationship.

Guilt and Anger in the Transference

Obviously if the analyst/therapist is serving a self-object function that past important figures in the patient's life failed to play – people who betrayed the child by becoming rejecting, abusive figures – the anger and rage provoked by that situation will be manifested in the interaction with the treater. How overt, intense, and direct these negative transferential feelings toward the analyst/therapist will be depends a great deal not only on the specific traumatic experience and ways the patient managed the trauma psychologically but also on the treater's capacity to tolerate and metabolize the patient's emotions. The patient may try to force the analyst to identify with her projected past negative object relationship, whereby the therapist becomes the bad, abusive figure as mentioned previously. Otherwise, the patient could distort and misinterpret the treater's intentions and find validations in the analyst's comments of perceived actual or latent rejection and revictimization no matter how accurate the interventions may have been. The rage resulting from past experience contaminates the relationship to a point that only by maintaining an empathic, introspective position and resisting identifying with the patient's massive projections will the therapist be able to gradually decrease the contamination of the therapeutic relationship by the past traumatic ones.

Frequently, the transference reactions are displaced away from the analyst, and it then becomes the responsibility of the treater to refocus the patient back to the transferential relationship, to find a resolution to the internalized/projected conflict and to prevent further deterioration in the patient's interpersonal relationships apart from the treatment situation. Again, aggressive feelings and thoughts as verbalized in the treatment sessions should not necessarily be viewed as secondary to frustration of the patient's infantile longing and wishes. These are appropriate emotions for someone who was traumatized as a child and is perhaps having a first opportunity to verbalize her feelings. The patient will gradually correct the distortion within the transference and the intensity of the emotion will decrease, aided by the therapist's ability to help the patient contain and digest her feelings. A new reality emerges that permits the subject to experience self and others differently. The quality of the self-relationship will improve and translate into an overall improvement in the patient's object relations.

Guilt reactions can be activated by the transference and at times can be one of the main manifestations of distress within the transference. It is not unusual to detect overt guilt feelings connected with the beginning of the resolution of the patient's traumatic experience. Improvement and psychological growth are linked in many of our patients' minds with negative feelings. Since the attempt at becoming autonomous was interfered with, the child may have grown up with a feeling that separating and being herself was wrong. Many patients report dysfunctional, symbiotic parents who felt threatened by the child's attempt at assertiveness and individuation, responded by withdrawing affection and devaluing of the child's capability. The result is a feeling of anger and guilt generated by the faulty parent–child relationship. This can manifest in the transference as well with the generation of guilt and anxiety in the face of psychological growth. At times, it can be seen clearly how guilt pushes the patient back, as if the only way to alleviate feelings of guilt, anger, and anxiety is by self-sabotage and return to a dysfunctional state.

Dreams and the Therapy of the Trauma Victim

Dreams have classically been considered as an excellent vehicle for accessing the unconscious mind of the analysand. Freud's qualification of dreams as "the royal road to the unconscious" is self-explanatory. Dreams are useful tools in any psychoanalytic treatment, though the importance of the dream as the royal road has lost ground. Most analysts now consider dreams as another piece of psychological material to be scrutinized and analyzed, no more equal in importance than any other memories, feelings, or thoughts emerging in the context of the psychoanalytic process.

Dreams are helpful in working with victims of childhood abuse. At times, dreams can give the first clues to past trauma and can aid in the recovery from trauma. Dreams are overdetermined, condensed, disguised, and have multiple layers of meanings. They must be interpreted taking into account a variety of factors, such as phase of treatment, therapeutic alliance, timing, and current events in the life of the patient, to be employed to full advantage.

What is of crucial importance in working with dreams in general is the patient's capacity to associate to different parts of the dreams and the role of the patient's elaboration in uncovering a theme and aiding in accessing repressed memories.

Mrs. G. was interested in getting an evaluation to decide whether her state of anxiety was caused by her current job-related stress or whether there was a deeper psychological problem that deserved formal psychotherapy. The first session was devoted to learning about her life history and obtaining more details of her symptoms and character orientation, and recommending the best way to proceed. She agreed to several evaluation sessions. In the second hour, she reported a dream that she described as a nightmare. She was with her father in a bathroom, where they were being threatened by three men;

she felt her father was going to be killed if he did not comply with their demands (it was unclear what they wanted from him or her); she felt she needed to do something to save her father's life and escaped. Her association revived her memories about having been raped together with two other friends in their early teens by a man threatening them with a knife on a Halloween night. She felt afterward she could have done something to prevent the rape; she felt guilty and unrealistically responsible for what happened, even though she recollected having a knife to her face. She remembered and wondered about the meaning of the number 3 (three men holding her father, three girls being raped by the perpetrator); the need to protect others and the guilt for not preventing the event appeared to have helped in the recollection of the memory through her association, which led to an early exploration-evaluation about how that trauma might be contributing to her current state of anxiety.

In this particular case, the dream of a very psychologically minded patient helped from the beginning to identify the trauma and guide treatment recommendation; more important, it aided in the recovery of a vital piece of information from the patient's past.

OTHER PSYCHODYNAMIC APPROACHES

Psychodynamic approach(es) can range from highly expressive, transference-focused interventions, with predominant use of interpretation, as is the case with a highly extensive psychoanalytic therapy, to interventions that make relatively limited use of transference issues and interpretation, as is the case with supportive therapy. In between, there are a wide range of combinations of interventions, such as clarification, confrontation, and suggestion, alternating with several degrees of transferential phenomena and reality-based interventions. That hybrid combination of interventions constitutes the so-called supportive-expressive psychotherapy.

As a general rule, it can be said that the more expressive the therapy, the more frequent the sessions. Psychoanalysis is more intensive and consists of almost daily sessions; an exclusive supportive therapy takes place about once per week, with the supportive-expressive modality ranging from two to four sessions per week.

Whether a patient can benefit from one of these psychodynamic approaches in the continuum from highly expressive to a basically supportive modality should be based on indepth knowledge of the patient's strengths and weaknesses, identified during the evaluation process.

DIFFERENCE BETWEEN SUPPORTIVE AND EXPRESSIVE PSYCHODYNAMIC PSYCHOTHERAPY

Several factors help differentiate the highly expressive therapies, which we will divide into psychoanalytically oriented expressive psychotherapy or psychoanalysis, as opposed to the purely supportive, middle-of-the-road, supportive-expressive psychotherapy.

The chart in Table 5–1 illustrates both the different emphases and uses of technical interventions that differentiate the highly expressive therapies from the more supportive types.

PSYCHOANALYSIS AND PSYCHOANALYTICALLY ORIENTED EXPRESSIVE THERAPY

Psychoanalysis is not the most frequently indicated modality of treatment in working with adult survivors of physical, sexual, or

TABLE 5–1. Factors that differentiate psychodynamic approaches

Technical Factor	Psychoanalysis	Highly Expressive Therapy	Supportive/ Expressive	Supportive
Use of transference	Most frequent	Frequently used	Less frequent	Infrequent or never used
Use of interpretation	Always	Frequently used	Less frequent	Infrequent or never used
Therapist neutrality	Always maintained	Very frequently maintained	Less frequent	Much less
Use of other insight-producing intervention (clarification/ confrontation)	Occasionally used	Sometimes	More frequent	Frequently used
Reality based intervention (direct advice, guidance, orientation)	Never used	Very infrequent	More frequent	Most frequently used
Use of free association	Highly frequent	Occasionally	Less frequent	Never used
Use of couch or sofa	Always	Occasionally	Never	Never used
Frequency of session	4–5 times/week	3 times/week	1–2 times/week	1–4 times/month
Emphasis on insight	Always	Always	Frequent	Much less
Focus on symptom relief	Less frequent	Sometimes	Frequent	Most frequent
Emphasis on character change	Always	Frequent	Less frequent	Never used

emotional abuse in childhood. However, the clinician trained and skilled in the psychoanalytic field may identify patients with a history compatible with trauma who could benefit from an analytic approach. At times, this particular patient population presents an atypical manifestation of the trauma in combination with other psychological conflicts that may be related to the trauma itself but have been internalized, disguised to such a degree that only a highly expressive therapeutic process can facilitate their uncovering. In fact, as we have pointed out, Freud's initial thinking about the origin of the neurotic conflict was embedded in a theory of trauma during the childhood.

> Ms. B. came to the office seeking help for panic episodes that were increasing, which several other therapists had unsuccessfully tried to help her control. She was a bright, educated, young college graduate who experienced episodes of depression but who had always been able to meet the responsibilities of her job. Her internal turmoil grew worse in spite of supportive therapy and medication prescribed by other therapists and reached a climax when she suddenly became suicidal. Following a brief hospitalization and upon completion of a battery of projective psychological testing, a past traumatic event was suspected. On further exploration in individual therapy, she was able painfully and slowly to recover early memories of sexual abuse she suffered from her father. She was repeatedly sexually molested and fondled from age 3 to age 5 as recalled in her expressive therapy.
>
> Ms. B. has been in supportive-expressive psychoanalytically oriented psychotherapy with a frequency of two to three times per week. She is also considered a candidate for psychoanalysis, as she has shown an increased interest in pursuing her therapy on a more intense and frequent basis. Not only is she interested in symptom relief, but she wishes to have a more indepth understanding of the impact of the trauma on

her overall psychological functioning and to improve the quality of her life. Her psychological curiosity constitutes a desirable rationale for psychoanalytic treatment that goes beyond the working-through of the trauma.

Merton Gill (1954) defines psychoanalysis as "that technique which, employed by a *neutral analyst*, results in the development of the regressive *transference neurosis* and the ultimate resolution of this neurosis by techniques of *interpretation* alone" (p. 771).

The aspects of the analyst's neutrality, the intensive use of the transference, and the use of interpretation are clearly the most important ingredients of a psychoanalytic process. Ticho (1970), in "Differences between Psychoanalysis and Psychotherapy," identifies other aspects pertinent to our patients not included in Gill's definition:

1. "The goal of psychoanalysis is to obtain a thorough personality change in the patient"; the "overall goal of psychotherapy is the resolution of symptoms and the attainment of some degree of behavioral change."

2. Countertransference (in analysis) "is much easier to control because of the neutrality and relative inactivity of the analyst."

3. "The fact that the analyst does not gratify [infantile longings] . . . but instead interprets them . . . is by necessity experienced by the patient as frustration."

4. Psychoanalysis "cannot be limited ahead of time. Psychotherapy may be limited for a variety of reasons."

5. The area of investigation "of psychotherapy is limited while in psychoanalysis . . . [it] is unlimited" (pp. 128–138).

Psychoanalytically oriented therapy and psychoanalysis have specific indications for the treatment of trauma victims, provided that the patient is not in the acute phase of the trauma where other interventions could, perhaps, be more effective.

THE SUPPORTIVE PSYCHOTHERAPIES

As we have discussed, there is a continuum from psychoanalysis, the most highly expressive therapy, at one extreme, to the supportive (whether brief, focused or long-term) psychotherapy at the other end of the psychodynamic spectrum.

Freud was the first to use a supportive (and brief) approach. As early as 1906, Freud successfully treated the right-arm paralysis of the conductor Bruno Walter in six sessions (Sterba 1951), using a combination of direct advice, suggestion, and ego support.

What does supportive therapy support? Many trauma victims can make very good use of a variety of supportive measures. Various mental structures need support at different points during treatment. These may include ego support to encourage the patient's executive function, id support to encourage the therapeutic use of the patient's dormant assertive-aggressive capacity, or superego support to facilitate control and regulation of impulses and self-esteem. The therapist should be aware of what aspect of the mental structure is being supported or is in need of supportive interventions in order not to lose sight of the therapeutic goals when using this approach.

A variety of technical interventions are currently used in supportive and supportive-expressive psychotherapies, such as clarification and confrontation, which are insight-producing approaches. Non-insight-producing interventions include suggestion, advice, direct recommendations, persuasion, reassurance, educational or instructional intervention, and encouraging or prohibiting specific types of behaviors. In general, these non-insight-producing interventions are avoided in the more expressive modalities of therapy.

Whether the chosen treatment modality is supportive or expressive, short- or long-term, and whether the patient is psychologically minded or not, there are therapeutic barriers to be dealt with and crossed for the therapeutic process to move forward. Very frequently these barriers are present at the outset. Usually, they are related to the mistrust generated by the internalized past and the poor quality of object relationships, which continues to exercise control over the patient's feelings and behavior. The patient–therapist relationship is a caldron where the vicissitudes of the patient's past object relationships are played out. Fears of rejection or of being taken advantage of, fears of exploitation and renewed victimization are in the forefront of the beginning of any therapeutic process.

There are always two types of patient–therapist relationships. The real, uninterpreted relationship, which is like any other relationship, and the transferential relationship, which is dominated by fantasies and expectations on the part of the patient and usually evolves into the so-called transference neurosis. The latter may become a therapeutic barrier when it results in a transference resistance. With either type, in working with trauma victims, there will always be a need on the part of the patient to discharge built-up anger and rage generated by the insult to his or her self-integrity and the self-fragmentation that usually follow such a severe injury.

Techniques used to facilitate the discharge of emotions include (1) exploring feelings in connection with the trauma; (2) helping the patient to identify specific feelings connected with the abuse and to attach the emotion to a specific situation; (3) helping the patient abreact or discharge the feeling; (4) encouraging the patient to verbalize the affective reaction, which leads to a working-through of the traumatic experience and a resolution of the symptoms that brought the patient to therapy. In other words, the ego is no longer being attacked from inside, obviating the need for defensive operation and leading to a decrease in symptoms and behavioral problems. Whether a supportive approach works better than an expressive approach will be determined only by the patient's character and capacity to work in therapy and by the therapist's ability to uncover all the factors detailed in chapter 2 about the evaluation process. Either way, the goal is the same, that is, a resolution of the trauma, an increase in the patient's level of functioning, and an overall improvement in the patient's quality of life.

Definition of Different Types of Interventions and Description of Techniques

Interpretation is a procedure in which the latent meaning of what the patient says or does is brought out. From a technical point of view, interpretation is what is conveyed to the patient to help him reach the latent meaning of the unconscious material. The rules of interpretation, such as depth, type (transference interpretation, interpretation of resistances), and order of interpretation, are dictated by how the treatment is being conducted, which phase the treatment is in, and how ready the patient is to receive a particular type of interpretation. It is the psychoanalytic intervention par excellence.

Facilitation is the provision of verbal and nonverbal cues that encourage the patient to continue talking. Examples are nodding one's head, leaning forward in one's seat, and saying "Yes, and then . . ."

Reflection is a technique in which the therapist repeats to the patient, in a supportive manner, something the patient has said. It lets the patient know that the therapist is actively listening to and understands the patient's concerns.

Clarification aims at helping the patient become more aware of obscure factors, usually below the level of verbalization, which are relevant to the treatment process. The therapist clarifies the patient's feelings, for example, when he shows the patient that what is being described as fatigue is actually an expression of depression or when he demonstrates to the patient patterns of behaviors or typical ways of reacting to certain situations. "Clarification does not refer to repressed or unconscious material but to factors that escape the patient's attention but that he can readily recognize when they are presented [clarified] to him" (Bibring 1954, p. 746).

Confrontation refers to the demonstration by the therapist of contradictory verbalization or behaviors on the part of the patient; it opens up new ways of exploring the patient's conflicts and creates more self-awareness.

As previously mentioned, these varieties of therapeutic interventions should be tailored to the patient's needs, time-appropriateness, and type of therapy.

The shifting back and forth from a supportive to a more insight-producing intervention, as is frequently seen in patients treated with a supportive-expressive psychotherapy modality, presents a clinical and technical challenge to the therapist. The blurring of the boundaries with such a combination of interventions will tax the clinical skills of the therapist in ways not frequently experienced in formal psychoanalytic process or in straightforward supportive therapy situations.

6

Cognitive and Behavioral Treatment Strategies

COGNITIVE STRATEGIES

Introduction

A trauma will have an impact on cognitive development as well as on any other developmental current. The severity of impairment in the cognitive sphere will be dictated by the specific developmental phase the victim of childhood trauma is going through. Any interference of the patient's cognitive maturation may affect the overall organization of the individual's perception of the world, with serious consequences for the internalization of object relationships and the separation–individuation process.

Piaget's (1963) basic concepts of mental schemata and the processes of assimilation, accommodation, and equilibration will be reviewed in the context of their relationship to transference phenomena and pathological states derived from physical, sexual, or emotional abuses. How a trauma may interfere with the well-known cognitive developmental phases, as first described by Piaget, will be explored. Emphasis is made on the inability of the organism's mental apparatus to accommodate new environmental stimuli into previously formed, affectively charged, and trauma-related mental schemata to explain some of the clinical phenomena seen in work with trauma victims.

Piaget's Theory of Cognitive Development

Piaget explains four concepts basic to understanding the processes of intellectual organization and adaptation. These are (1) mental schemata, (2) assimilation, (3) accommodation, and (4) equilibration.

Mental Schemata

Piaget believes that in the same way living organisms have different biological structures that permit their physiological functioning, the mental apparatus comprises structures he calls schemata, which help the individual organize environmental stimuli. At birth, schemata are mostly reflexive and can be inferred from motor activities such as sucking and grasping and coincide with Piaget's first phase of cognitive development, called sensory motor intelligence, which operates from age 0 to age 2. Schemata change with the growth of the organism and its development through the life cycle.

Assimilation

Assimilation is a constant cognitive process by which a child integrates new perceptual matter or stimulating events into existing schemata or previously integrated environmental stimuli. Assimilation accounts for the growth of schemata, although it neither changes their quality nor influences the development of different schemata.

Accommodation

Accommodation is the process by which new schemata are created or modified. It allows stimulation from the environment to be assimilated in different concepts or categories. To clarify the difference between assimilation and accommodation, it can be said that assimilation describes the forced fit of stimuli to the person's structure or schemata. Accommodation describes the reverse. The person is forced to change his schemata to fit the new stimuli. Another way of putting it is that accommodation fosters qualitative development and assimilation accounts for quantitative growth. Together these processes account for intellectual adaptation and the development of intellectual structures.

Equilibration

What Piaget meant by equilibration is a necessary balance of cognitive growth and development during the processes of assimilation and accommodation. These processes, which result in the development of new cognitive structures, are actively operating throughout the different phases of cognitive development, starting with the sensory motor phase, followed by preoperational thought, concrete operation, and finally the period of formal operation. Other factors mentioned in Piaget's cognitive theory are maturation, physical experiences, social interactions, and motivation.

The affective state of a trauma patient could very well play a role in the development of cognitive structures and vice versa; a particular mental schemata could color the individual's perception of a given situation and the emotional reaction stemming from it. The perception of an event (whether traumatic or not) can contaminate and alter the affective state of a person. Further complicating the clinical picture are primitive defense mechanisms such as projection and splitting, which are frequently very much active in different stages of childhood development. It is conceivable for a child to develop different mental schemata out of similar situations since other factors, different from the cognitive/perceptual capacity of the child, may enter in the formation of a specific mental schemata. Factors such as the affective state of the individual, quality of defenses against anxiety, and degree of ego growth, among others, are significant. As the child grows, the impact of these factors is minimized; as the ego matures, healthier defenses begin to operate; as the maturation of the central nervous system progresses, the forces of reality allow the child to organize experiences in a less distorted way; reality is accommodated in different, new, more adaptive mental schemata.

Clinical Implications of Piaget's Cognitive Theory in Relation to Work with Trauma Patients

Developmental Aspects

The interrelation between structural development and Piaget's theory of cognitive development can be seen more clearly when we look at the development of the mental structures such as the ego, superego, and ego ideal. Even though it cannot be postulated that development of ego and superego depends only on object relations or cognitive development, these two lines of development are extremely important and probably have a profound influence on the quality of both superego and ego functions, common areas of impairment in trauma patients. Self-assessment; self-perception; reality testing; judgment; the capacity to think abstractly, to observe one's behavior, and to be self-critical; assertiveness; self-esteem; and self-image—are all clearly connected with an internalization of values and norms of behavior via imitation and identification with important objects in the life of the individual, aided by the development of schemata throughout the process of assimilation and accommodation of these different environmental stimuli. The adult survivor of childhood trauma has distorted mental schemata particularly concerning self-relationships and self-perception. These schemata are like frames of references or index cards: stimuli in interpersonal relationship are compared, assessed, and either integrated as part of an already formed ego structure (assimilated) as is usually the case with trauma patients; or the number of index cards is expanded (accommodated) to promote ego growth and a more accurate perception of reality as part of the normal process of development.

Viewing ego–superego functions from this angle makes it easier to understand how the multitude of stimuli from the environment perceived by an individual create multiple mental schemata, where different norms of behavior and value systems and moral standards can be incorporated. These mental structures can thus help the individual compare, assess, judge, and make decisions according to the schemata previously developed. Distorted mental self-schemata, the result of traumatic events in the life of a child, crystallize into dysfunctional ways of perceiving or relating to oneself and others. An individual's psychological capacity normally continues to grow throughout life as realistic schemata continue to develop; using a cognitive approach in work with trauma patients allows the necessary changes and modifications to outmoded schemata that lead to behavioral changes.

Cognition and the Concept of Transference

Technically the concept of transference in the psychiatric literature refers to the phenomenon of reacting to the analyst with feelings, thoughts, and wishes as if he or she were someone from the patient's past. The therapist/analyst is not immune to this clinical phenomenon. In the course of psychotherapeutic treatment, unconscious feelings are revived and infantile strivings are reactivated in an attempt to find gratification via transference. In other words, the trauma patient (and this applies perhaps to any other patient) is forcing the environmental stimuli (assimilating a contaminated perception of the therapist's behavior) into an archaic schema related to the experience of the trauma. The strength of the repressed affect may also play a role in this pathological process. It is widely recognized how the impact of emotions affects the perception of reality. Primitive affect appears to have primacy over cognitive organization, although it can be argued that cognition prevails in terms of being able to exercise some degree of control over the affective state. Emotional states may either facilitate or hinder cognitive development as well as distort reality by forcing new stimuli to be assimilated into outmoded schemata. The reverse, that is, cognitive distortion provoking different affective states is also true. This is an issue that has profound technical and clinical implications when working with trauma patients.

The resolution of the transference reaction in trauma patients, as well as the resolution of superego projections, can be viewed in Piagetian terms as the development of a new schema, that is, the representation (accommodation) and assimilation of the therapist/analyst as a different, real person, compared with the archaic, primitive figures of the perpetrators of the abuse(s).

In working with trauma patients who have developed a mental schema that forces them to perceive reality in a distorted way, the treater must find ways to help the patients modify their cognitive styles by facilitating the formation of new schemata or facilitating the accommodation of previous negative perceptions. A new "index card" is formed so the patient can assimilate or internalize new experiences through the working relationship with the therapist that will translate into more adaptive behavior and more acceptance of himself and others. The concept and process of internalization in object relations theory and the process of formation of new schemata via assimilation and accommodation are closely related. Both translate into a better quality of object relationships, new identification units, stronger ego identity, a toned down superego, and increased self-esteem and better capacity to relate to oneself.

The process of organizing the environment based on different schemata may be primordial to the development of character structure. The infant will interpret reality on the basis of what he already knows. The Rorschach test is probably based on the same premise—that the individual will reveal his existing psychological structure by the way he interprets the reality of the inkblot; in other words, he will interpret the projective tests based on what he already knows, and what he has internalized. In the same way trauma patients interpret the current environment based on their past experience, which often leads to conflict. An individual's knowledge of present or past reality should not be considered, and is not, a duplicate of the "objective" world, since each person develops or constructs a different understanding of reality; what trauma patients believe to be true at the beginning of treatment, they later realize, as they modify their cognitive impairment in treatment, was a dramatic distortion of the actual reality. Here, we agree with Slap's (1987) claim that perception "is not an inherent ability for exact, photographic registration of the external world" but is "dependent on [schemata] which are affected by past experience, psychodynamics, affective state and cognitive style" (p. 629). In Piaget's words, "Knowledge is not transmitted directly but is constructed"; and he adds, "There are no innate structures; every structure presupposes a construction" (Piaget 1967, pp. 149–150). Therefore, knowledge (whether it fits or not with the past and present) is an evolutionary process that originates in every individual based on personal experience with the environment. The reciprocity between knowledge and its continuous interaction with the environment has a profound influence on the way character develops in psychopathology and the way trauma patients deal with their problems.

Cognitive-Oriented Techniques in Work with Trauma Patients

The mind first perceives an event (perception is an ego function) and later gains knowledge about that same event by the intellectual process we call cognition. But knowledge can also remain in the unconscious, as in the case of a repressed memory. The evaluation of a reality event is a cognitive act; the way one experiences that reality event is what is called affect. Trauma patients most frequently have a distorted perception of traumatic events and frequently that perception translates into an irrational belief or interpretation of what happened to them earlier in their lives. Intimidation and threats by the perpetrator of the trauma and the tendency to blame the victim for what happened (since many of the victimizers portray themselves as benefactors, teachers, or simply doing the victims a favor) results in the formation of a mental schema of the event that may be totally divorced from the actual happening.

Ms. A. showed difficulty, from the beginning of her therapeutic process, in giving herself credit for any of her accomplishments. Though she was a high-functioning, productive individual, she had a very devalued perception of herself; as her therapy progressed, she became aware of emotional neglect and sexual abuse she had suffered. She remembered how her mother used to devalue her and how she was forced to believe she was unworthy. As she began to verbalize her anger at the parental abusive figure, the stage was set to begin modifying her self-perception and her cognitive style of self-blame and self-inhibiting and guilt-laden behavior. As the therapy process went on she became aware of her need to submit and to please others, a situation that made her dependent on others' unpredictable behavior, as she had been in her relationship with her own mother. As she recapitulated some of this past behavior with the therapist, she had the opportunity to look at the irrational way she had interpreted her previous experiences. Modifying an archaic, distorted mental schema from a negative self-representation to a more positive self-image translated into a resolution of the transference reaction and a gradual discharge of aggressive feelings and rage, and an overall improvement in her capacity to relate to herself and others. To put it in structural terms, there was a toning down of the rigid superego, a decrease in ego–superego tension, and a strengthening of the ego capacity to adapt and to function.

A first task of the therapist is to correct the mental schemata by putting blame where it belongs. This is usually followed by an attempt to match appropriate affect with the traumatic event and the facilitation of abreaction. Irrational interpretation of the event by the victim and the inability to accommodate it will gradually diminish as the cognitive distortions are chipped away. The knowledge patients acquire about themselves and about the traumatic event that brought them into therapy should progress from the intellectual sphere to that of the affect, and become an emotional experience. Overt emotional display commonly precedes further structural rearrangements as the perception of the internal world of the victim changes with the discharge of emotions. Unconscious knowledge or repressed memory first ought to become conscious before any mental distortion can be elicited and it is a prerequisite to make any affective bridge with the cognitive counterpart. Whether the patient is engaged in an exploratory uncovering via a psychoanalytically oriented process or whether the patient already has full awareness of the trauma, helping the patient discharge the appropriate affect is crucial to the healing process. Once the patient acquires the knowledge and begins to correct the cognitive distortions, many of the trauma-related interventions and techniques reviewed in chapter 7 become increasingly more important.

BEHAVIORAL STRATEGIES

Introduction

The behavioral premise that anxiety and fear are direct by-products of the perception of danger argues for the application of classical behavioral theory to treatment of adult survivors of childhood emotional, physical, and sexual abuse. Accordingly, the traumatic event(s) that besieged our patients form the basis for a conditioned, psychologically distressing response (physical, emotional, and/or behavioral) to certain stimuli. The associations to the original stimuli made by the victim broaden the cues (triggers) to which the patient applies avoidance behaviors as a means of escaping or decreasing symptomatology. As the avoidance behaviors continue to increase, memory becomes more deeply buried, specific symptomatic aftereffects are reinforced and create complex dysfunctional behavioral patterns, and psychological treatment becomes more complex and, therefore, more difficult.

Behavioral therapy has an important role in the treatment of survivors. Its advantage is that it allows the psychotherapist to address certain symptomatology by implementing appropriate behavioral techniques relatively quickly and easily, thus bringing expeditious relief to the patient. The proper application of behavioral strategies instills within the patient a renewed sense of hope, often in the initial sessions, thereby increasing motivation for treatment.

Behavioral theory literature documents the efficacity of combined interventions that target a specific symptom compared with the exclusive application of any single strategy (Deffenbacher and Suinn 1987).

As discussed in chapter 1, it is clear from the psychological literature concerning adult survivors that frequently these patients manifest a variety of generalized and specific psychiatric symptoms. For example, they may present in treatment with complaints of excessive anxiety and fear, depression, psychosomatic problems, difficulties in interpersonal relationships, self-destructive behaviors, sexual dysfunction, and posttraumatic stress disorder (PTSD) symptomatology, among others. Some individuals also exhibit the additional problem of learned helplessness, with problem-solving and coping skills (behaviors) that are typically passive, deficient, and ineffective.

Accordingly, the psychotherapist might include behavioral management techniques in the beginning and middle phases of treatment, as they are well suited for dealing with many of the above-mentioned symptoms. While it is believed by many clinicians that such an approach tends to be efficacious in providing short-term relief and, in some cases, long-term relief, if appropriately applied, it also affords the therapist time to implement many other technical interventions, discussed throughout this book, that promote long-term results.

In addition to accomplishing temporary relief of symptoms, behavioral techniques contribute to the patient's sense of empowerment relatively quickly, a vital by-product of these interventions and desirable for adult survivors who have been struggling with feelings of helplessness and loss of control. Other benefits include an increase in the individual's repertoire of effective coping skills and contributions to restoring self-mastery over one's life and environment, with an attendant increase in self-esteem and self-confidence.

There is a belief among some therapists that the working alliance in behavioral therapy is impersonal. The cold, detached attitudes sometimes thought of as permeating this therapeutic approach are inappropriate in the treatment of adult survivors.

When employing behavioral interventions, the therapist needs to establish a positive rapport with the patient in order to effect the desired psychosocial changes. Such personal growth may not occur absent a solid foundation of trust, caring, acceptance, and empathy in the therapeutic interpersonal matrix.

Surely, the therapist needs to be aware, before teaching or prescribing any of the following behavioral strategies, of the patient's psychological readiness, level of motivation, and commitment to do the homework between sessions consistently. Further, it is recommended that the shaping of the patient's new behaviors be accomplished by stressing one achievable step at a time until the ultimate goal is reached. The psychotherapist can use positive reinforcement to encourage the development of these new behaviors while concurrently teaching the adult survivor the skill of positive self-reinforcement in order to assist the patient in becoming autonomous.

There is, of course, a wide spectrum of behavioral strategies; it is not within the scope of this book to discuss all of them. However, we have included the following behavioral management techniques, which we have found to be most effective and potent when combined with other psychotherapeutic approaches set forth and described in this book. In short, behavioral therapy can be an integral part of our multidimensional approach to the psychological treatment of adult survivors of childhood abuse.

Thought Stopping

Many survivors have obsessive victimizing thoughts that are both negative and destructive, resulting in unpleasant feelings that may also lead to dysfunctional behaviors. Among these repetitive thoughts are self-doubt and self-criticism, conflicts with others, fear of making decisions, and negative performance evaluations about self and the future. These patients also experience intrusive thoughts from the trauma episodes consisting of obsessive memories related to the perpetrator's verbal humiliation and abuse, and excessive criticism and/or self-destructive thoughts.

The thought-stopping technique involves the therapist teaching the patient to focus on the negative thought for a few seconds and then thinking the word *stop* to interrupt the chain of dysfunctional thoughts. Next, it is important for the patient to substitute a positive or functional coping statement and think it over and over again. If the negative thoughts are too intrusive and/or resistant, it may be useful for the patient to wear a rubber band around a wrist and gently pull it, while at the same time, thinking *stop*, and then replacing negative thoughts with the positive voluntary thought, thinking it over and over again.

This technique works relatively quickly if initially practiced by the patient five to seven days a week, over a period of a few weeks. The patient will need to repeat this process as soon as destructive, negative thoughts begin. Even though there may be an occasional recurring thought remaining, typically the patient will experience a substantial diminution of the problem.

Journal Writing

Despite a few limitations, journal recording has been shown to be another helpful strategy for survivors while they are undergoing psychotherapy for both abuse-related or non-abuse-related issues. Naturally, a patient needs to be consistent as well as self-motivated to properly obtain benefits from this therapeutic tool, since most of the work for them takes place outside of therapy sessions. Patients who present in treatment with extreme verbosity or affect as well as those with difficulty verbalizing orally to the therapist (primarily related to fear reactions) may be desirable candidates for this particular procedure.

A variety of a patient's needs can be met through this writing process. Initially, the extent of their anxiety (or other symptoms) can be reduced, even though in some cases the relief may be temporary. In our experience, the recording process may ameliorate the extent of ruminative thinking experienced by the patient.

Journal recording provides a valuable account of abuse- or trauma-evoked memories, thoughts, affect, beliefs, physiological sensations, experiences, and so on. Depending on the patient's needs, this material can be explored, validated, facilitated, challenged, interpreted or enhanced alone or shared, in part or whole, with the clinician. It becomes her chronicle of the therapeutic treatment process. As the patient writes down what was once experienced in the past, she can begin to identify important themes, defenses, patterns of behaviors and feelings, and to become aware of how some present difficulties or symptoms are related to past childhood experiences of trauma. Writing allows the patient to discharge formerly repressed emotions and thoughts in a safe context. This procedure can also teach the patient to contain and, perhaps, to process intrusive memories, flashbacks, dreams, and distressing associations while concurrently using the journal as a medium to recall buried recollections. Frequently, it can provide emotional relief as well as an opportunity for the patient to learn to gain control over her psychological material, particularly between therapy sessions or if other support systems, including the psychotherapist, are unavailable. In other words, it is a procedure that can enhance the patient's ability to calm, contain, and soothe herself.

It should be noted that patients who find it difficult to verbalize the highly charged past abuse–related material with their therapist can record the threatening recollections in order to open up to their fears without feeling too vulnerable. At some later time, however, the patient needs to be encouraged to share the traumatic material.

Relaxation Training

There is a high likelihood that many victims of childhood abuse will manifest symptoms of PTSD, anxiety, overwhelming fears, panic attacks, or psychosomatic problems. Individuals who have "forgotten" their traumatic past may initially present a delayed disorder in therapy, or it may be triggered at any point during treatment. Therefore, it can be very helpful at that time or prior to the onset of

By learning to become assertive, the survivor is able to deal more effectively with all kinds of people and situations, thereby creating an opportunity for desensitizing previously conditioned anxiety and/or fear responses. Additionally, patients will enhance their self-confidence and self-esteem and increase their autonomy and initiative while concomitantly contributing to their self-efficacy. Above all else, assertiveness gives to adult survivors a sense of empowerment to become their true selves.

7

Abuse/Trauma
Treatment Strategies

TREATMENT PHILOSOPHY

Several basic philosophical principles provide the foundation for treatment of adult survivors. Although these concepts are of paramount importance when treating these patients, it is critical to draw on a wide spectrum of other valuable principles inherent in the mental health field, which are likewise reparative when appropriately employed.

Perhaps no other principle is more fundamental in working with survivors of childhood abuse or trauma than the nonblaming approach. This may be the tenet that underlies all other abuse-focused concepts and values. Clearly, it is the essential ingredient enabling patients to eventually liberate themselves from their learned victim role. The therapist helps the patient assign responsibility definitively for the abuse to the adult violator and to assuage the blame wrongly attributed to the child victim. That the adult brings to the relationship with a child both more power and life experience, as well as know-how, is widely supported in the literature. It is, therefore, axiomatic that it is the adult who is accountable for any abuse(s) resulting from that power differentiation (Sgroi 1988).

Another valuable tenet of abuse-focused theory is the notion of depathologizing. This principle is that aftereffects resulting from the abuse of the victimized individual are not viewed as pathological behavior but are conceptualized as typical reactions to an abnormal event. In other words, the symptomatology is not labeled a pathological process per se but is viewed as the result of what was available to the child as survival tools (Briere 1989). For example, hypervigilance in everyday living is commonly deemed to be a pathological symptom. Abused children, nevertheless, often develop hypervigilance as a means of avoiding danger. Whereas such behavior would seem maladaptive years later in adulthood, it was crucial for their survival at the time of the threat.

The clinician must be keenly sensitive to the essential principle of individualized treatment. Each adult survivor is a unique individual, and because each problem is specific and different from any other, the therapist's approach must be suited to the patient's personality, needs, capacities, desires, opportunities, and motivations. This reality challenges the therapist throughout the course of treatment. The failure or refusal of the therapist to remain fully cognizant of these myriad distinctions will result in a disservice to the patient. This principle is employed by the therapist who functions from a nonbiased, nonprejudicial stance; who applies knowledge of human diversity; who listens and observes to enhance better understanding of the patient; who moves at the patient's pace; and who empathizes with the survivor. Illustrative would be a situation in which two children are victims of substantially similar acts of emotional abuse. The impact on each of them might be so different that, whereas one might require many years of intensive psychotherapy in adulthood, the other might emerge largely unscathed, with minimal symptomatology. As each of our patients is different from all others, the appropriate treatment should accordingly be individualized (Sgroi 1988).

Establishing and maintaining a safe, caring, and trusting therapeutic relationship is a principle of primary importance. It is vital that the therapist be aware that in implementing any skill or technique with adult survivors, the primacy of the therapeutic connection that makes possible all interventions cannot be over-emphasized. Although many of the abuse-oriented treatment strategies are the curative tools that, skillfully applied, will achieve the patient's goals, they will fall short of complete success without a "good enough" relationship between therapist and patient. Thus, the therapeutic alliance is the most potent force that influences, facilitates, and enhances any and all of these methodologies.

Also, as discussed in prior chapters, the unique value of the complex therapeutic relationship is that it leads to a corrective emotional experience, with concomitant positive changes in terms of promoting ego growth and improvement in relationships with others.

It is important for the clinician to recognize that his or her belief in the disclosures of abuse by these victims is an additional core treatment philosophy central to the patient's healing process.

In some cases, survivors have had the incidences of their abuse or trauma disbelieved or ignored by others. Other victims suffered silently, not willing to take the risk inherent in disclosure (Lister 1982).

Reports of adult sexual abuse in the literature maintain that well over 99 percent of all complaints made by children against an adult are accurate. In his classical essay, "The Child Sexual Abuse Accommodation Syndrome," Roland Summit (1983) states that of the infinitesimal number of misstatements made by alleged victims,

> most had sought to understate the frequency or duration of sexual experiences, even when reports were made in anger and in apparent retaliation against violence or humiliation. Very few children, no more than two or three per thousand, have ever been found to exaggerate or to invent claims of sexual molestation. It has become

a maxim among child sexual abuse intervention counselors and investigators that children never fabricate the kinds of explicit sexual manipulations they divulge in complaints or interrogations. [pp. 190–191]

The failure of the therapist to respond to the victim/survivor's recitations of the acts of abuse without empathy and sensitivity will most likely have a profound impact upon the patient, even to the extent of revictimizing him. Such disclosure(s) to the therapist generally flow from a sense of confidence and trust in the clinician. We believe that this will result in the professional serving as a catalyst for the patient's feeling a sense of safety in the therapeutic matrix, permitting him to reveal additional details of the trauma necessary for healing.

As noted by Sgroi,

the reaction of the person who receives the disclosure may be an important variable influencing the impact of the sexual abuse on the individual. For instance, we believe that a supportive and believing response from the person who receives the child's disclosure can be very helpful to the victim. Alternatively, a nonsupportive reaction can be devastating. [p. 145]

The final crucial precept of our treatment philosophy is the empathic approach. It should be apparent that empathy is an integral part of our work with adult survivors of childhood abuse. It is woven through the fabric of the entire treatment process. An empathic style will substantially increase the chances of successful treatment; lack of empathy will most likely prove counterproductive. According to Carl Rogers (1961), the eminent psychologist, "The therapist is experiencing an accurate, empathic understanding of the client's world as seen from the inside. To sense the client's private world as if it were your own, but without ever losing the 'as if' quality—this is empathy, and this seems essential in therapy" (p. 284).

SPECIFIC ABUSE-RELATED TREATMENT STRATEGIES

The selection of the appropriate technical treatment interventions for patients obviously will vary depending on a wide variety of circumstances discussed in chapters 2 and 4. The treatment strategies and techniques we have discovered to be the most efficacious, as well as those suggested by others from experience in the field, are discussed below.

Naturally, interventions that might be highly effective when used by one clinician might be totally ineffective, or worse, if attempted by someone incapable of successfully implementing them. Surely, this is no criticism of a psychotherapist who by virtue of personality is ill suited for a particular intervention; it is, however, a caveat. The therapists must possess heightened self-awareness of and insight into their own character organization. In short, they need to choose and implement interventions from this and subsequent chapters that are compatible with their individual styles and strengths.

NORMALIZING

One of the most dynamic and indispensable techniques, in terms of restorative benefits, involves "normalizing" the survivor's abuse-related symptomatology.

Typical of the psychological mechanisms employed by the survivor is negative introjection. Commonly, this is manifested by self-accusation or self-deprecation, which is used to characterize and justify the childhood incidents of abuse trauma. "I must have done something wrong to deserve . . ." or "There is something wrong with me" permits the survivor to rationalize and tolerate his or her own victimization. Some patients believe they are intrinsically pathological because they were subjected to these deleterious events. Patients frequently exhibit feeling of shame and guilt, and believe simultaneously that they are different and distant from everyone else.

It is important that, at the appropriate times (see Chapter 4), the psychotherapist reframe the patient's current survival behaviors as understandable reactions to abuse in childhood. Also, by explaining to the patient, "What happened to you was wrong, but there is nothing wrong with you," the therapist reinforces the accurate perception that there is nothing inherently wrong with the patient. Thus, the clinician sets in motion a process for destigmatization (Finkelhor and Browne 1985). To distinguish between the event (the abuse/trauma) and the victim (the patient) enables patients to normalize their accommodation response. It enables victims to decrease their reliance on such abuse-related coping mechanisms while making it possible for them instead to utilize more adaptive or functional behaviors.

Additional useful corrective statements include "Because something bad happened to you, doesn't make you bad," "These are expected aftereffects of having been abused by a perpetrator(s)," or "Because something awful happened to you, doesn't mean you are an awful person." Most likely, these will assist patients in reappraising themselves, others, and the abusive event, and ultimately in separating the trauma from both their self-concept and self-esteem.

One caveat must be mentioned in connection with this technical intervention. The psychotherapist needs to remember that successful corrections of survival beliefs and defense mechanisms are frequently slow, often depending on a clinician's steadfastness as well as his or her ability to repeat the strategy throughout the treatment process before the transformation is integrated by the patient.

REATTRIBUTION OF SELF-BLAME

When working with adult survivors, perhaps the most powerful treatment strategy is correcting the cognitive schema of self-blame. The therapist's reframing of this erroneous belief becomes the core of many profound changes for the victim, both intrapsychic and interpersonal.

It is essential for the clinician to keep in mind some of the multidimensional aspects of the cognitive distortion of self-blame. Initially, many of these patients were told by the perpetrators that what happened to them was their fault. In some cases, they even may have been "rewarded" for their involvement, which reinforced their belief that they were responsible. Such brainwashing, coupled with the effects of the trauma may, in some cases, result in terror and overwhelming confusion, causing the child to doubt his or her reality.

Another factor that contributes to self-blame is the frequent tendency and need for secretiveness due to the lack of a safe environment for disclosure. Also, unable to cope with an almost total loss of control, the child will revert to feelings of intense guilt and shame. In order to survive, the child will create an illusion of control, of which denial is a significant factor, and often continues to trust the offender rather than lose the ability to place trust in anyone.

Inherent to a child's coping skills is the belief that he or she lives in a just and fair world and that safety is no further away than her significant others. When victimization occurs, and the child is unable to find safety or restitution with such significant others because that they are either the perpetrator or an enabler, the child's world is shattered. The child is left with no alternative but to attribute the trauma to her own making.

As discussed in Chapter 4, the reframing of self-blame cognitive distortions generally leads to what seems to be, for a period of time, a mixed blessing. Though the survivor is feeling a lessening of guilt and shame, other repressed memories with their concomitant intense emotions will begin to surface. In other words, the patient may appear to have become more symptomatic and, therefore, worse. Sometimes patients will manifest intense emotions including rage, terror, despair, pain, feelings of abandonment, as well as being out of control or going crazy. The clinician must clearly convey to the patient that the powerful affect experienced now is a delayed reaction to the past trauma events. The adult survivor needs to realize that she can take control of herself in the present and is now experiencing feelings that are overwhelming the child within. This explanation is vital; while the child within is experiencing these emotions, the adult can remain in control and grounded to reexamine the trauma material using current cognitive powers and successfully integrate it.

EXTERNAL AUXILIARY EGO INTERVENTION

In chapters 3 and 4 we stated that the issue of self-blame either creates or exacerbates insidious and innumerable problems in terms of the patient's self-esteem and self-concept. The therapist must aid in the development of the patient's true self, particularly during the beginning and middle phases of treatment.

Initially, the therapist needs to pay full attention to elements that must precede the implementation of this intervention. First, to allow for the unfolding of the self-object transference (Kohut 1977); second, the patient must be psychologically ready to benefit from a positive intervention—timing is essential; and third, the intervention needs to be adaptable to the personality and treatment orientation of the clinician.

Within the context of these elements, the therapist must serve as a self-object to the patient in order to help repair the survivor's self-esteem deficit. This will be accomplished only if the therapist accepts, affirms, and validates the patient unconditionally; demonstrates a genuine and nonjudgmental interest in the patient; validates the patient's feeling states as appropriate to the victimization; confirms and assures the patient of his or her intrinsic worth and lovability as a human being; validates the patient's strength in having survived the trauma; consistently validates the patient's perceptions; encourages and validates autonomous behaviors. These therapeutic experiences will pave the way for the internalization by the survivor of the good, affirming, and validating object to facilitate the patient's ego growth.

INNER-ABUSED CHILD-WORK UTILIZING PATIENT'S CHILDHOOD MEMORABILIA

In our experience, it has become apparent with most patients that the utilization of childhood memorabilia such as photographs and home movies provides a therapeutic tool that has a fourfold reparative effect. The attendant benefits are:

First, from photos taken prior to the victimization, the patient can reconnect with who she or he was pretrauma. For example, a 30-year-old female patient recently located an early childhood photograph hidden away in her attic. Even a cursory view of that long-forgotten family portrait immediately brought her to tears. The impact of that picture probably could not have been duplicated by any other means. The patient observed herself in early childhood, prior to the onset of abuse by a housekeeper. The full smile on her face seemed to be radiating the internal happiness and security that was then hers. Familial love and caring permeated the scene. The patient had known a safety, joy, carefreeness, and warmth that would soon be eroded. The patient poignantly recalled, for the first time in twenty-five years, the life that had been hers. She was now able to begin to work on the psychological issues emanating from the loss of that life.

The therapist's multiplex task in the above example was to maintain a safe therapeutic matrix while simultaneously reflecting and validating any verbal and emotional responses by the patient. This promotes the patient's reconnection with his or her true self. At other times, the therapist can facilitate the open expression of feelings by the patient. Additionally, the survivor needs to be encouraged to notice and verbalize the differences before and since the abuse, by asking them open-ended questions related to the photograph(s) and, perhaps, sharing some of his/her own observations and impressions in terms of the dissimilitarities before and after the abuse.

When discussing the photographs with the patient the following are suggested questions from which the therapist can select:

Tell me, what do you see in this photograph?

What do you notice about yourself when you look at the photographs (face, body, others)?

What do you look like?

What expression is on your face? In your body? Any physical sensations?

How do you feel now as you look at yourself in that photograph? Toward others?

What feelings are expressed in that photograph?

What qualities or personality traits did you have when this photograph was taken?

What do you like about yourself in the photograph? Feel proud of?

What beliefs did you have then about yourself, others, the world?

How do those beliefs compare to the beliefs you have today about yourself, others, the world?

Is there anything in that photograph that would relate to the way you are today?

What meaning does this photograph have for you now?

Did you learn anything about yourself or others from this photograph?

We have likewise found it beneficial to request that patients find and keep a pre-trauma, specially framed photograph that they like and attempt to reconnect the child within with that image of themselves at an earlier age. By expressing, affirming, and feeling unconditional love, acceptance, and respect for the child within, that patient can (re)establish the sense of wholeness and continuity injured by the trauma.

Second, the patient will now be permitted a self-view at the time of the trauma. The following case illustrates the above-mentioned effect.

> In working with a middle-aged male, who had previously been in therapy for many years with another psychotherapist, it was noted that he suffered from an assortment of psychosomatic symptoms. He manifested many indicators of childhood abuse, but insisted to the clinician, as he had to his former one, that he had lived an idyllic childhood. When it was discovered that he had access to early childhood photographs, it was suggested to him that he share them in therapy. The photos belied his memory; the expression on his face in the photos portrayed a reserved, unhappy, and frightened youngster who clearly did not represent the patient's recollection.
>
> Because of the psychotherapist's empathic attunement and unconditional acceptance of the patient in that photo, he no longer found denial necessary and accepted the reality of his abuse, which subsequently contributed to the patient's own self-acceptance.

Third, the patient can retrigger the cognitive and affective memories of the past traumatic event from the photographs. Some adult survivors have repressed much of their childhood experience related to their victimization. Their childhood photograph(s), therefore, can become a catalyst in facilitating their ability to recall the multifaceted circumstances surrounding their abuse. While working with survivors, we have observed the surfacing of psychological sensations such as numbing, shaking, aches and pains, and so on, as well as both repressed cognitive and affective memories ranging from subtle to intense.

> Jacqueline, a 32-year-old survivor, initially sought treatment because of difficulty containing her aggressive impulses toward her husband, and difficulties in her interpersonal relationships with both men and women.
>
> At the request of her therapist, the patient produced a photograph of herself at age 15 in her first prom dress. While discussing the physical and emotional abuse she had suffered at the time of the photograph, for the first time she had a specific recollection of being the victim of sexual abuse by her father. The image of her blossoming sexuality retriggered her memory of having been victimized by him; feelings of intense anger, disgust, and fear emanated from her.

The therapist's position should be supportive and accepting while bearing witness to survivors' recovered past horrific experiences in order to validate their reality.

Fourth, the patient can observe the sequelae of the trauma. Patients can bear witness to the pictorial reality of their past, including pre-abuse, the abuse itself, and post-abuse. The evidence of the trauma is often clearly observable on the face and body of the victim; occasionally, it is even observed upon others portrayed in the photographs.

Jacqueline, the patient discussed above, was startled while reviewing a photo album by the difference in her affect as she pored over photographs of her which taken during the three phases of her life. As she viewed the happiness and joy in her pre-abuse years, she recalled herself as a vibrant, gentle, precocious, and pretty young girl. The apparent contrast, evidenced by the photos taken during the period of her abuse, caused her to realize the enormous impact the trauma had had upon her. The image that she had brought into therapy with her, that of her being ugly, shamed, quirky, and tough were now understood by her to be aftereffects of the abuse. The moment of truth swept over her as she grasped the significance of what was before her.

The additional task of the clinician in the above example was to promote the patient's capacity to draw the vivid comparisons between the photographs of the past and the patient today. The questions previously listed can be appropriately asked by the psychotherapist at this time. Additional questions may help the patient to make comparisons between the three phases of the abuse (pre-, during, post-):

Do you see a difference in yourself in photographs taken pre-, during, or post-abuse? What are the differences in you during each of the phases of the abuse (trauma)?

Can you remember any sights, sounds, smells, or tactile sensations?

What feelings did you have in any of those photographs that you no longer have, if any? Did you have any physiological reactions to those feelings?

What feelings evident in those photographs do you still have today? Are you able to soothe yourself?

As determined by the photographs, what are the differences in you between the times depicted in the photographs and today?

TRAUMA MEMORY AND/OR
RECONSTRUCTION WORK

The cornerstone of psychotherapy with adult survivors of childhood abuse/trauma is the successful reconstruction, resolution,
and integration of the traumatic material by the patient. Psychotherapy with these patients is not limited to the traumatic event(s)
per se.

Childhood trauma can have a maladaptive psychosocial rip-
pling effect on its victim. An avoid-and-recall or ebb-and-flow
characterizes a pattern in which treatment of the primary traumatic
reconstruction material alternates with treatment of both nonre-
lated symptomology or secondary aftereffects from the trauma.
Danieli (1989) states, "Indeed, when psychotherapy dwells on certain periods in the survivors' lives and neglects others, it hinders
survivors and their offspring from meaningfully recreating the flow
within the totality of their lives, and may perpetuate their sense of
disruption and discontinuity" (p. 439).

The therapist must continuously maintain the safe psychotherapeutic matrix while at the same time using all of the therapeutic
principles and skills in his or her repertoire. The reconstruction of
the trauma is laborious psychological work for the patient and
constitutes perhaps the therapist's most difficult challenge. In order
to avoid harmful consequences, proper pacing of the patient's
material must be adhered to throughout the process.

We need to be our patients' most trusting, empathic, and
healing ally so they will permit us to accompany them in the
descent into their unconscious, in the hope of helping them extri-
cate themselves from the noxious ties that bind them.

The process used to accomplish this goal is complex, as the
explanation that follows indicates.

The triggering or evoking of traumatic memories, both affective and cognitive, will vary from patient to patient. The memories
can be disturbing or bearable, fragmented or whole, and vary in

intensity from a brief flash to a flood. They can vary in duration from a few seconds to a few hours and may range in type from superficial to profound. For some patients, the memories are triggered spontaneously from sensory stimuli within the environment, including smells, tastes, sights, or sounds that were present during the trauma and became associated with it. Other patients' buried memories are evoked by various life stressors: anniversaries, times of crisis, dreams, or perhaps a life situation that in some way resembles the original abuse. Sometimes patients have only vague memories, and the therapist tries to facilitate the reactivation of memory process by employing one or more psychotherapeutic techniques, such as childhood photographs or other memorabilia. Art therapy is also useful—patients might draw pictures of themselves as children in whatever memory fragments they have of the trauma.

Initially, patients will reexperience one or more facets of the trauma. They must verbalize what and why it happened to them in as much detail as possible, including descriptions of the sensory impressions associated with the trauma and accompanying feelings. At this point, it is sometimes desirable for the therapist to validate and bear witness to the patient's recall and to demonstrate empathic attunement by verbalizing to the survivor insight-producing clarification or supportive intervention, such as a reflection.

Next, the clinician needs to encourage the patient to recount any recollection of physiological memories by asking the patient, "Did your body respond?"; "Describe how it did"; "What did it feel like?" Encouraging the patient to reexperience the body memories will facilitate the patient to discharge them, allowing them to eventually fade away. One caveat of paramount importance: Psychotherapists must be extremely cautious when victims of sexual abuse describes their physiological reactions or responses in positive terms. In such instances patients may have an abiding sense of guilt, having concluded that any gratification they felt constitutes an indictment and makes them bad or responsible. Clinicians have the delicate task of explaining and normalizing these body sensations, distorted cognitions, and feelings so that victims will ultimately be able to distinguish normal physiological human reactions from the responsibility for the trauma.

The therapist must encourage and help patients to talk about their behaviors during and after the abuse by asking: "What did you do during the abuse?" "After the abuse?" This will assist the therapist in making an assessment of the psychological defense mechanisms and other survival tools utilized by a patient.

The therapist also needs to facilitate description by patients of what they thought about during the abuse by asking: "What were you thinking during the abuse?" "What meaning did the abuse have for you, if any?" "Did you tell yourself anything else during the abuse?"

Further, the psychotherapist must help, encourage, and guide patients to reexperience, identify, openly express, and integrate the variety of feelings related to the trauma. This will help them to discharge emotions, thereby decreasing their intensity and ultimately solving the problems that resulted from them. The therapist needs to validate patients' reactions by stating, for example, "This is an understandable response to being victimized by another person," or "You don't have to feel guilty because someone victimized you," and/or "Your feelings are understandable reactions to being abused."

Now as childhood memories have become more vivid, ordered, relived, reexamined, and assimilated, patients can place them in the past and begin to assess how they impacted on and affected their lives. It is important that appropriate connections be made between childhood experiences of abuse and adult dysfunctional behaviors. Additionally, the therapist assists patients in the reappraisal of past malevolent cognitive schemata in order to establish current benevolent ones with a new perspective, new understanding, and new meaning of themselves and their world.

GRIEVING THE LOSSES OF THE TRAUMA ("TIERS OF TEARS")

In many cases, atrocities of childhood abuse leave adult survivors with profound traumatic losses. The magnitude of the injuries sometimes surpasses the level of tolerance of the human psyche. To describe this phenomenon of losses as "tiers of tears" gives us insight about how this process impacts its victims, both directly and indirectly.

The multidimensional aftermath is responsible for losses almost too numerous and pervasive to detail. Accordingly, we list below many of the types of losses experienced by victims.

Losses of Security

safety
control/power
trust
world view, (just, fair)
protection
peace
spirituality
certainty
comfort
continuity
rootedness
predictability

Losses of Childhood

innocence
play
joy
spontaneity
flexible roles
freedom
choices
memory
youth
childhood

Losses of Self

empowerment
esteem
identity

Losses of Others

attachment
healthy, trusting relationships
good family – nurturing

confidence	good parenting
efficacy	social skills
independence	meaningful relationships
opportunities	siblings
potential (self-growth)	peers
intellectual	adult
emotional	intimacy
social	
physical	
sexual	
occupational	
spiritual	
financial	
integrative	
creative	

Obviously, the material in the list is not intended to be all-inclusive. In some cases, additional losses will be evoked as a result of the insidious effects of the primary loss. At times, other losses that the survivors experience may be the by-product of the interaction of one loss upon another. In short, the losses caused by childhood trauma both initial and secondary, can be of such a nature and variety that they may be extremely difficult to isolate and identify. As Judith Herman writes (1992), "The telling of the trauma story thus inevitably plunges the survivor into profound grief. Since so many of the losses are invisible or unrecognized, the customary rituals of mourning provide little consolation" (p. 188).

Grieving, as with most issues, varies in both intensity and duration. Patients may grieve for weeks on end or only for several minutes a session.

Because so many survivors were inhibited from expressing their feelings as children, they experience marked difficulty in exhibiting those feelings after many years of repression. Consequently, the release of the affect is often interrupted, titrated, sporadic. It becomes all the more essential that the psychotherapist provide those elements, noted in chapters 3 and 4, necessary to facilitate patients' open expression of emotion, in particular, grief.

The clinician's task in working with adult survivors in their mourning process is multiplex. Initially, the therapist needs to guide and help patients identify the losses so they can fully acknowledge and understand them. Once patients accept the reality of their traumatic past and their inability to alter it or undo it, the mourning process unfolds. It is a particularly arduous time for the patient and requires a great deal of therapeutic skill and sensitivity by the clinician.

Surely it is imperative that the patient feel and give full expression to all of the psychological responses to the loss(es). Therefore, the therapist needs to encourage this expression of feelings by demonstrating interest and by utilizing appropriate and timely interventions so that the patient can begin the emotional process of unburdening. For some survivors, another focus is to assist them in the development of safe and useful skills to express these overloaded grief-related feelings between sessions. Among the means that the therapist can suggest to the patient is to record or express feelings through the use of journal-keeping, creative writing, and art work (see Chapters 6 and 8).

In the grieving process, some patients experience a multitude of fears such as uncontrollable crying ("crying forever"), being destroyed, and appearing "weak." We have found it efficacious to gently challenge those distorted beliefs, without being judgmental, by assisting patients to substitute corrective and functional beliefs for troublesome ones.

It is time for patients to reinvest their emotional energy into other facets of their lives, lives that now offer opportunities to reach out for new relationships and challenges. Each patient's program will not be seen as a metamorphosis, but an integration of the new with fragments from the past.

The therapist's task is to facilitate patients' establishing new intimate relationships or rejuvenating others, encouraging their involvement in developing new interests and forging new lives. Survivors will require guidance and support from the therapist, since the world from which they have emerged has, to a large extent, ceased to exist. No longer will abuse of power triumph, will secret lives be treasured, will patients feel stigmatized and helpless. The opportunity for a renewal of life is present and it is the psychotherapist who can provide assistance and encouragement to patients to capture the moment.

The emotional energy largely consumed by the grieving process is now replenished and available to be redirected to pursuits of patients' choosing. With the support of the therapist, at this phase survivors will be ready to reinvest their energy. This may include establishing new goals, creating a new meaning and perspective, restoring the ability to reconnect with themselves, others, and the world in more profound and intimate ways, all of which will permit patients to transcend their past and become thrivers in both the present and the future.

8

Adjunctive Therapies

INTRODUCTION

Given the complexity of the diverse aftereffects experienced by adult survivors of childhood abuse and trauma, the utilization of a multimodal approach is indicated. The vital role that adjunctive therapy may assume in the healing process of the patient cannot be overemphasized. Given the broad scope of the impact upon the victim, appropriate treatment modalities will generally vary in number and type depending on the biopsychological and sociocultural deficits of the individual as assessed by the psychotherapist.

Surely, it is not our purpose in this book to present each of the many adjunctive therapies in depth; we will, nevertheless, examine several of those with which we have had much success.

PSYCHOEDUCATIONAL

It is not surprising that many of these patients are likely to present in treatment with multifaceted deficits in coping skills characterized by poor problem-solving strategies, inadequate basic life skills, and insufficient general education information.

Actually, many patients have developed high levels of survivor skills, yet may have sacrificed developmental skill building, thus failing to develop those abilities necessary to function effectively. Treatment, therefore, should first focus on an individualized evaluation of the patient's strengths and deficits by the therapist and then on goal setting with the patient to increase his or her overall coping skill repertoire.

In our clinical experience, we have found while working with adult survivors that most of them begin psychological treatment with many misconceptions about childhood abuse, its aftereffects, and other related symptomatology and by-products. We have seen that most patients benefit significantly from an increase in an understanding of the complications and factors resulting from and perpetuating their problems.

The aim of this section is to provide the clinician with specific information related to this life-enhancing component of treatment for the adult survivor patient. The clinician needs to be aware that the information presented herein is an addition to psychotherapy, not a substitute for it. The following are of particular importance.

General Education Information

Abuse/Trauma-Related Information

As we have documented in prior chapters, childhood abuse exists in epidemic proportion and is deeply woven into the fabric of our society. It is essential that patients be apprised of these facts and develop an awareness of the problem and its ramifications. Awareness translates into a gradual decrease of the denial and other psychological defenses employed by survivors, and provides the basis of the understanding and acceptance necessary for patients to begin to explore their plight.

This material is readily available in the form of books, movies, newspaper and magazine articles, audio- and videotapes, as well as lectures. Such resources can be useful in lessening feelings of isolation, shame, and guilt, especially when they describe the experiences of other adult survivors of childhood abuse.

Social/Relationship-Building Skills and Intimacy Issues

Intimacy is viewed by the victim as a frightening experience, and becoming close with others is frequently seen as dangerous; everyday relationships are difficult. Survivors often times have experienced childhood mistreatment from significant others in the form of violation, betrayal, manipulation, exploitation, and rejection. In some cases, these early and continuous abusive interpersonal experiences translate into a chronic withdrawal from life and others. Unfortunately, these victims develop both a sense of vulnerability and a fear of relating to other people and tend to retreat from others in relationships. Often, they perceive the world as a lonely and unsafe place. Patients may present in treatment with feelings of alienation, loneliness, and sadness.

It should be noted that their narrow range of social skills may be related, in part, to their dysfunctional childhood caretaking role or any other rigid, fixed past role. Such a deficit can limit and shape the choice of behaviors learned in early relationships, and victims develop a narrow range of effective social skills.

Interventions by the therapist should be aimed at assisting the survivors to rise out of their isolation and destructive interactions with others. Also, treatment needs to focus on increasing the relationship skills repertoire so that patients have a variety of strategies at their disposal.

If appropriate, patients can be helped to risk reaching out, establishing and maintaining constructive relationships, and learning adaptive social tools that will develop knowledge, insight, and understanding of themselves and others. These skills include effective communication and assertiveness training, the ability to express feelings appropriately, reciprocity in relationships, and appropriate self-disclosure. Most important perhaps are the role interactions within the therapeutic relationship, which can also facilitate the acquisition of these abilities by the patient. Therapeutic conditions such as trustworthiness, empathy, unconditional positive regard, warmth, and authenticity consistently demonstrated and modeled by the clinician can assist the survivor in developing such capacities.

By understanding the relevance of social expertise to their lives and by practicing and applying it, skills will develop and social connections will increase, promoting healthier relationships and fostering a sense of satisfaction and self-fulfillment.

Body-Image Information

Generally, adult survivors struggle with a distorted body image manifested by expressions of personal dissatisfaction with their bodies and by self-destructive behavior, for example, eating disorders, drug addictions, and self-mutilation.

Early dysfunctional life experiences often are a significant factor in contributing to a negative body image. Past maladaptive family attitudes, beliefs, abusive experiences, and unrealistic concern about a child's appearance and bodily functioning, tend to overfocus victims' attention on themselves and may lead to a nonacceptance of their physical selves. The sociocultural milieu, with its unrealistic attitudes, beliefs, and perfectionist expectations of men's and women's body shape and size, also contributes to the problem of a negative preoccupation with one's physical stature.

Treatment by clinicians can focus on helping victims increase their knowledge and understanding as well as create a sense of self-control with these issues, assisting them to break out of their negative perceptions. The therapist can also help patients to increase their awareness of distortions of body image by clarifying associations between a devalued body image and their abusive childhood experiences. It is also useful to educate patients about the sociocultural, personal, and familial influences that tends to result in survivors becoming more aware of the combination of factors that have influenced their perception of their body. Further, the utilization of therapeutic art activities, photographs, body movement, corrective posture body imagery, and visualization strategies are typically valuable for modifying body disparagement common in survivors of childhood abuse and especially in sexual abuse victims.

Sexuality Issues and Sex Education

Childhood abuse and, in particular, childhood sexual abuse can frequently adversely affect the sexual functioning of the adult survivor. For some patients, the belief that their self-worth is determined by being sexual and taking care of others is a salient issue. Such survivors typically have distorted both their cognitive beliefs and their views of sexual norms. They might have advanced sexual experience, yet may be rather ignorant about their own bodies.

Some victims tend to act out sexually, which may contribute to compulsive sexual involvement, indiscriminate, numerous sexual partners, and/or sexual preoccupations; while at the other extreme, some patients might avoid sexual contact and manifest sexual difficulties such as sexual inhibition, arousal problems, low or nonexistent sexual desire, or fear of sex. Problems with achieving orgasms or erections, flashbacks, numbing or pain during sexual intercourse, or feelings of guilt, shame, or anxiety during sex are all too common with some survivors.

The primary goal is for patients to regain control over their sexuality and, at the same time, take a healthy sense of pleasure in their bodies. Within a supportive, sensitive, and validating therapeutic relationship, it is most important for the therapist to provide accurate information concerning human sexuality to the patient, thereby reducing confusion relating to the human reproduction system and its functioning. Also, information concerning birth control and sexually transmitted disease – AIDS, in particular – is very useful to the survivor. Many misconceptions resulting from abuse or trauma can be significantly modified with factual information and can diminish feelings of guilt and fear, for example, an understanding of the body's normal physiological responses to sexual stimulation.

The clinician needs to explore the patients' attitudes and beliefs about their sexual abuse at the patients' own pace. Appropriate discussions with victims about the many common sociocultural myths, individualized to a patient's specific situation, can be extremely beneficial in reducing feelings of stigmatization while improving self-esteem.

Exploring the past abusive or traumatic relationship(s) with patients in terms of what it afforded them, the variety of feelings it evoked in them (pleasurable and unpleasurable), and sexual questions it provoked within them, helps patients to clarify and ventilate the many issues that have burdened them.

Additionally, the therapist assists patients to identify and reformulate their disturbed cognitive beliefs; helps them to recognize and express their desires, needs, and preferences in sexual interactions; and permits patients to sort out the differences between sex, love, affection, and attention.

Parenting Information and Skills

Since adult survivors have often been exposed to significant dysfunctional parenting, it is advisable for the clinician to assist the patient with the myriad of parenting issues they may be dealing with. Part of the therapeutic task is to work with these individuals to help them develop functional parenting skills and provide them with effective child-rearing information.

Frequently, adult survivors are very concerned with the effect of their parenting on their own children. Many important questions are raised by victims about their parental role, communication style, discipline strategies, family structure, boundaries, and general responsibilities. In some cases, patients are experiencing a loss of control, confusion, anguish, and anger about the behavior of their children. Another task of the clinician is to assist them in coping with the problems of their children by enabling them to gain a better understanding and insight of the situation, thereby empowering them to function in their role as parents in a more self-confident manner. Additional focus on teaching patients how to strengthen the parent–child relationship and exploring alternative options for dealing with parental responsibilities is also suggested.

Basic Life Skills

Effective Communication Skills

Typically, survivors enter psychotherapy exhibiting marked difficulties in the area of communication. Many victims lived in families with impaired communication patterns and were probably more likely to communicate nonverbally or in dysfunctional styles. They lack the ability to express themselves clearly, are unable to ask directly that their needs and wants be met appropriately, and often cannot resolve conflicts satisfactorily.

Most adult survivors benefit significantly by improving their communication skills. The psychotherapist should both assist and encourage patients to build this pivotal ability, which may form the basis for new achievements and relationships. In addition to acquainting the patient with these skills, modeling them as an essential aspect of the therapeutic relationship can also help survivors to develop expertise.

Treatment will usually involve helping patients to develop

active listening skills, appropriate affective expression, expression of open, clear, direct verbal "I" statements, and conflict negotiation and request making, among others.

Boundary and Limit-Setting Skills

Victims of childhood trauma often come from unstable home environments where personal boundaries were clearly violated. They have difficulty with establishing healthy limit setting, which results in these survivors feeling unsafe, distrustful, insecure, and confused. Many had no opportunity to develop a sense of empowerment or choice. Personal safety and body rights were not a given.

It is important for the clinician to provide a safe forum for the patient to explore and test out alternative behaviors. It is in this secure, healing, growth-promoting environment that the victim finally can have an opportunity to develop personal rights, power, and controls, and make autonomous choices. Clinical interventions are focused on promoting an emotional atmosphere in which patients feel liberated and safe to learn in healthy, respectful ways the power of saying no to the therapist and others they encounter. Survivors can also create boundaries by developing separate interests and creating independent activities, verbally expressing their ideas, beliefs, feelings, and so on, and getting their needs met in relationships.

Problem-Solving and Decision-Making Skills

Because their problem-solving and decision-making skills are impaired, adult survivors are in an especially vulnerable position. Typically, these patients were not taught or given appropriate opportunities, during the formative years, to enable them to develop effective means to cope competently with the daily problems of life.

These patients need to be instructed by the clinician in the principles of problem solving and decision making in order to help them adapt to any daily difficulty or other life situation. The therapist needs to monitor subsequent sessions to examine and re-evaluate with patients his/her progress in implementing these strategies for possible refinement of this tool.

Other Basic Life Management Skills

It is similarly apparent that the development and enhancement of patients' coping skills will increase the probability of achieving goals. While this pursuit is sometimes subjective and will vary accordingly from person to person, certain other basic life coping skills are seen as essential. Among those are prioritizing, time management, conflict resolution, anger management, and setting limits.

Family Therapy

Family therapy is not the treatment of choice for an adult survivor of childhood abuse or trauma for both obvious and subtle reasons; it is generally contraindicated. The patient typically comes from a pathological family system, and most members are not motivated to participate in family psychotherapeutic treatment sessions because of long-term family denial.

Unfortunately, the majority of these malfunctioning families remain unhealthy, characterized by the elements discussed in chapter 1, for example, a lack of clear boundaries, maladaptive communication patterns, closed system, role reversal, and use of marked mental defense mechanisms. As such, many of these family members are still destructive and might very well attempt to sabotage the therapeutic process. When some adult victims begin psychotherapy they decrease contact with their family of origin, if not already estranged, and gain psychological distance in order to develop a new and realistic perspective of both the family dynamics and their own unhealthy psychological coping patterns. They may reconnect in healthier interactions when feeling psychologically stronger.

In our experience, we have found that individual psychotherapy is the treatment preferred by many survivors, with or without group psychotherapy as a secondary therapeutic modality. It is, nevertheless, desirable for the clinician to be thoroughly familiar with when, how, and why family work may be indicated and beneficial to some adult patients. If family members are supportive, it would probably be advantageous to involve them in the survivor's treatment process to some extent.

One of the more difficult decisions the therapist may face is whether one or a series of sessions should be scheduled with the adult survivor and his or her offender(s). Further, if such a session(s) is desirable, what place, if any, should other family members have in conjunction with a process in which the victim confronts the perpetrator?

Such an arrangement must be made on an ad hoc basis. In determining what would be most healing for a patient, his or her ego strength must be assessed, as must the nature and extent of the formidable challenge to be undertaken. Clearly, the variables to be evaluated are many; the benefits and risks could be enormous. The decision, therefore, will take into consideration many complex determinants; the therapist's goal is to assist the patient.

Should such an encounter be deemed advisable, the mechanics and goals must be very well planned. The therapist must be prepared for any special problems or nuances that might arise. Among the considerations may be whether the contact should be direct or indirect, who will make contact, when and where and for how long. Does the patient have realistic expectations? Initial contact may be made with more supportive members of the family to bolster the patient's confidence; timing is also essential.

We find it vital that the patient be provided with a safe,

trusting holding environment (Winnicott 1965) for adaptive change. Accordingly, the therapist needs to be constantly vigilant to take whatever action is appropriate in the best interest of the patient. Our theoretical orientation regarding this special, limited family work has been influenced by Minuchin's structural family therapy, Satir's communications family therapy, and Bowen's family of origin therapy. The combined treatment approach we have developed provides patients a safe arena to think, feel, and behave in very different and more functional ways with their family of origin. Central to our view, the therapist serves as a facilitator in order to assist the patient to communicate more effectively with the other family members.

Group Psychotherapy

Although individual therapy is the keystone of the adult victim's recovery, it has also been determined that the group treatment approach can be a potent adjunctive component of the total therapeutic treatment process. It provides survivors with a unique opportunity to help ameliorate their psychic wounds. While there has been some disagreement concerning its role, group psycho-therapy has become a significant part of the overall treatment plan of patients who have a history of abuse or trauma. Since the group therapy milieu may lead to a reactivation of PTSD reactions or other psychological symptomatology for some survivors, we believe that it should be utilized only in conjunction with individual psychotherapy, where these problems can be treated more effec-tively.

The primary goals of the group experience are several: to see isolation evolve into intimacy with others, to establish trust in interpersonal relationships, to change powerlessness and helpless-ness into empowerment, and to transfor stigmatization into healthy self-esteem.

The group model provides an opportunity for survivors to have a substitute family, an environment within which a recapitulation of unresolved past and present conflicts can be safely reenacted. This permits a corrective emotional experience in which members can resolve boundary, sibling, role, communication, and parental issues, among others. Additionally, the group affords survivors another chance at testing out new behaviors, shedding old, rigid family roles, breaking dysfunctional family rules, and learning to create new supportive, reciprocal, intimate relationships, which will enhance patients and their world.

Other goals common to the clinical group experience may include decreasing feelings of shame, irrational guilt, and self-blame; developing hope for healing; learning functional skill building; and processing group transference issues.

Information regarding group formats, prescreening assessments, group composition, group facilitators, group themes, and other structure and process issues are available in other books and resources for reference. Careful attention to the techniques and mechanics of successful group psychotherapy in the treatment of adult survivors can prove to be a powerful vehicle for change and psychosocial growth.

Ancillary Programs and Therapeutic Activities

Self-Help Groups

Self-help or mutual aid groups have developed as a reaction to the needs of millions of people who are experiencing problems from an array of psychological, physiological, social, or spiritual arenas. Usually groups are created by members who have themselves successfully dealt with a particular problem and can be an important personal resource for others who share a similar plight.

These groups provide at no cost a twenty-four-hour support

network, emotional support, direct feedback, important informa-tion, tools, and guidelines for coping with a particular difficulty. Referrals to self-help groups for adult survivors may be a valuable adjunctive resource for some patients at some time during their therapeutic treatment process. Self-help groups can also facilitate interaction with nonauthoritarian peers, help decrease defensive barriers manifested by some victims, assist in addressing self-destructive behaviors, and can be an external source of motivation for some patients to make constructive changes in their lives.

Expressive Therapies

The creative art modalities have been gaining recognition as valu-able adjunctive treatment in healing for adult survivors. They can provide patients with an alternative to, or can be used in conjunc-tion with, the traditional verbal therapies for victims who are unable to discuss their traumatic material directly. Art, dance, writing, music, and drama are viable options to aid the patient in working through their abuse experiences.

Art Therapy

Many adult survivors of childhood trauma can benefit from the inclusion of art therapy into their overall psychotherapy treatment program. This modality provides a nonverbal, symbolic means of communication for the patient. When direct efforts at assessing or reviving unconscious memories or feelings become blocked, art therapy is one indirect approach that has frequently proved suc-cessful to achieve this aim.

Additional goals of this modality are to promote self-awareness and self-understanding, to discharge tensions related to the abuse or trauma, to resolve inner conflicts, and to deal with specific issues such as distorted body image.

Somatic Psychotherapy

Ever-developing and sometimes very useful techniques are those
that we describe as somatic psychotherapy. These therapeutic
modalities may be employed either in individual or group treatment. Especially well suited for the nonverbal patient, this approach permits patients to rediscover and reconnect with their
bodies, resulting in heightened self-awareness coupled with a sense
of liberation of their physical essence.

Ranging from dance or movement and exercise therapy to the
more placid body imagery, the goal is to connect the physical and
visual perceptions of the survivor with the psyche, often producing
both diagnostic and therapeutic success.

Other Expressive Therapies

Other expressive therapies that have proven valuable with adult
survivors are music therapy, psychodrama, creative writing, including poetry therapy, and sand play therapy. The goals that can
be attained by the effective use of expressive therapy include
improved communication skills, sublimation of impulses, experiencing of feelings as a highly valuable and powerful aspect of the
self, and working through traumatic material.

9

Clinical Complications in the Treatment of Trauma Patients

A variety of clinical complications may arise in working with victims of childhood abuse. In addition to the classical manifestation of posttraumatic stress disorder as described abundantly in the literature, patients at times show special problems that may require the use of parameters and modifications of previously described psychotherapeutic interventions. These include the use of hospitalization and medication for self-destructive tendencies, psychosis, or severe dissociative episodes.

The treatment process may reactivate or exacerbate preexisting nontrauma related conflicts. The uncovering and remembering of past traumatic experiences during treatment sessions could require the use of external forms of containment and control while patients are in crisis. Paradoxically, the safer the environment and the more solid the patient–therapist relationship is, the more the patient can afford to let go of previously established psychological defenses, however dysfunctional and maladaptive they may have been.

Patients may feel that for the first time in their lives they can safely verbalize their emotions and be understood. However, the intensity of the emotions and the full awareness of their feelings may be prematurely exposed and could lead to episodes of disorganization, extreme guilt, severe somatic or psychological reactions, or psychotic and dissociative episodes. Every patient is different and will require individualized and timely interventions.

We will describe some of the common complications seen in working with these types of patients. Among the clinical complications frequently seen are

1. acute depressive episodes
2. suicidal/homicidal behavior
3. addictive disorders
4. severe dissociative episodes
5. negative therapeutic reactions
6. other complications

When confronted with any of these complications, most of the time the clinician has to resort to the use of hospitalization for containment and limit setting. In such cases the use of neuroleptics and tranquilizers is often indicated; crisis intervention, multi-therapy interventions (group, individual, marital, family) are at times necessary to contain and prevent further emotional deterioration.

ACUTE DEPRESSIVE EPISODES

Most victims of childhood abuse suffer from different degrees of depressive symptomatology. A devalued sense of self, with a poor self-image and self-esteem is usually the case. As explained in previous chapters, the poor quality of object relationships leads to the formation of faulty ego–super ego systems that frequently are manifested in the form of irrational guilt. The formation of a pathological self-schema leads to cognitive distortion that also contributes to chronic depressive feelings. In the course of treatment, patients are likely to experience intense exacerbation of the depressive symptoms leading to acute depressive episodes. The clinical manifestation varies from patient to patient; classically the individual shows neurovegetative symptoms such as insomnia, appetite changes, fluctuations in body weight (anorexia or overeating), atypical somatic pains and complaints, lability of affect, and in extreme cases, self-destructive tendencies.

It is of extreme importance to prevent further deterioration in the patient's psychological state as the patient continues to work on the trauma issue that fueled the depressive episodes. However, the clinician may face a situation in which different psychological factors may have combined and crystallized into an internalization of pre-trauma conflicts that gave rise to the development of a depressive character structure, thus complicating the presenting trauma symptomatology. This is a situation that tests the clinician's skills but that may to some degree be anticipated if a good clinical assessment has been made prior to the initiation of the actual therapeutic work. The level of premorbid (pre-trauma) depressive symptoms can range from a dysthymic disorder (or depressive neurosis) to a major affective disorder such as major depression or a manic-depressive picture. The clinical approach and decision concerning appropriate intervention (neuroleptic medication, hospitalization, among others) must be based on a thorough evaluation of the patient's needs and strengths.

HOMICIDAL/SUICIDAL BEHAVIOR

Homicidal and/or suicidal ideation or plans are emergencies that require dramatic intervention on the part of the therapist. The paramount goal is to keep the patient alive and to prevent harm to the patient or to others. Hospitalization is usually the rule in either situation. It is not unusual to see in some patients a fluctuation from self-destructive tendencies and behavior to homicidal ideation. We believe that in every suicidal person there may also be a potential homicidal person. Suicide ideations are frequently motivated by a wish to "kill off" the internalized "bad" introject; when the conflict is "externalized" it can take the form of homicidal tendencies.

Most commonly the factor behind homicidal ideation is a surge of rage and aggression as patients begin to identify the source of their chronic pain and psychological suffering. As patients start the process of ridding themselves of irrational guilt and self-blame for the past trauma and as they perceive themselves not as the party responsible for their own suffering, but as victims, there is a surge of justified emotions. In some cases, the emotions could lead to active, conscious aggressive feelings toward the significant person(s) in their lives who either perpetrated the abuse or did nothing to prevent it. The therapist should play an important role in helping patients modulate their anger in a way that prevents their battered egos from being overwhelmed and fragmented by the emerging painful memories and feelings.

Patients should show clear evidence that they are capable of containing the emotional reactions to the therapy sessions and be reasonably able to reconstitute as they leave the office. At the first evidence of a lack of emotional and impulse control, the clinician should introduce whatever parameters are necessary to prevent regrettable expressions of aggressive feelings. The knowledge acquired during the pretreatment evaluation process should be the clinician's guiding tool in dealing with such emergencies.

Depending on each patient's unique characteristics and pattern of coping with inner emotions, the clinical picture can fluctuate from self-destructive tendencies, if the patient is still prone to self-direct aggressive feelings, to display of aggression and violence toward others. The modification of the self-blame, of the distorted mental schema, could surprise the patient's ego at a time when its capacity to control emotions and impulses may be impaired. Let us keep in mind that only a very small percentage of patients develop this complication while in active treatment; more patients are capable of discharging their emotions in an adaptive way with the help of the clinician. Nevertheless, interventions needed to keep this type of complication under control ought to be given priority over any other aspect of the patient's treatment. Once the crisis is over, the patient will usually reconstitute at a higher level of psychological functioning, and the therapeutic process can continue its expected course.

ADDICTIVE DISORDERS

At times, some adult survivors of different types of childhood abuse may develop as part of their chronic, maladaptive attempts at coping with the sequelae of the trauma different types and degrees of addictive problems.

Comorbidity of addictive and posttraumatic disorder are common. At times, the addiction is what brings the patient for evaluation and treatment, but after a thorough assessment the clinician may realize that it was a symptom related to a past trauma. However, an addiction could develop as a complication during the treatment of this type of patient.

Underlying or aggravating the addiction problem is a surge of memories and emotions that create an increase in the level of anxiety and tension with which the victim's ego has to cope. Patients at times manifest a tendency to use drugs or alcohol to alleviate the increased tension and in the process develop a psychological dependency and subsequent pharmacological addiction that in turn will require acute and dramatic intervention by the therapist. Depending on the severity of the problem, the clinician will have to choose among different parameters to prevent further complication (both physical and psychological) and deterioration of the patient's social, familial, and work-related capacities.

Hospitalization is frequently needed to detoxify and treat the addiction; the use of medication to prevent physical-neurological complications and adjunctive rehabilitation therapies ought to be part of the treatment of this frequent and serious problem.

IATROGENIC ADDICTION

These types of addictive disorders are the ones created by physicians who prescribe tranquilizers, most frequently benzodiazepine-type drugs, to treat what looks like an anxiety disorder. These are drugs with a high addictive potential. The anxiety and tension the patients experience are connected with the chronic conflicts secondary to the trauma, but the physician, unaware of the true source of the conflict, may try in vain to alleviate the patient's suffering with medication. Unfortunately, a common practice in medicine is to target a particular symptom, in this case chronic anxiety, with a drug, an antianxiety agent. In spite of the best intentions on the part of the unaware physician, the result is the unfolding or worsening of an addictive complication that will require specialized intervention to address the underlying problem and, needless to say, treat the newly created one. The need for a comprehensive evaluation prior to any prescribed treatment (pharmacological or otherwise) cannot be overemphasized.

SEVERE DISSOCIATIVE EPISODES

This group of disorders includes different degrees of alterations of ego states and fragmentation of the self. They may range from episodes of fugue states, depersonalization, and derealization to severe forms of multiple personality disorders. Obviously, the impact of the trauma itself could lead to the development of any type of dissociative disorder and be one of the cardinal manifestations of adult survivors of childhood abuse when they first seek help. The patient may present initially with this specific symptomatology, allowing the clinician to anticipate that during the course of treatment, episodes of a dissociative quality are likely to occur. However, when the patients in active treatment begins to exhibit alteration in ego function, with repercussions in their overall daily functioning, we consider it to be a complication of the therapeutic process.

The introduction of parameters may be necessary to prevent any additional injury to the patient's psychological or social functioning, and periods of hospitalization may be necessary to allow a patient to begin to integrate traumatic memories with the help of a controlled and predictable environment.

The therapist should not hesitate to enlist the help of other clinicians to aid in the clarification of the clinical picture and treatment of this kind of complication. Different modalities of group psychotherapy and medication are seen as adjunctive in the acute dissociative complication in work with trauma patients.

Dissociation

We take issue with the concept of dissociation in the context of a continuum going from a normal reaction to a severe disorder such as multiple personality disorder (Braun 1989).

Dissociation is not in itself a disorder or a pathological entity per se; it is a normal mental mechanism or psychological defense against anxiety early in life. It is unconscious, as all defenses are, and by itself does not meet the criteria for a separate disorder in the same way that projection and repression are not pathological entities early in life but could be manifestations of different psychotic or neurotic states in the adult.

Dissociation as a defense mechanism can be considered normal if viewed in the context of developmental theory as playing a role in specific developmental phases, in the same way splitting (no matter how insignificant the part of the mind that is being split off might be) is not considered a manifestation of a pathological process early in life when it is part of normal development. However, dissociation is not considered normal in the adult no matter how brief the episode of dissociation may be. An individual may have thought blocking, thought intrusion, problems with concentration or attention span, or may have episodes of daydreaming or a rich fantasy life that may disrupt attention and concentration. Those cannot be qualified as normal dissociation or as part of the normal side of a continuum leading to severe dissociative disorder.

In our view dissociation is an unconscious dynamic with a primary defensive role in the adult and reflects the existence of an underlying psychoneurotic disorder. Any clinician will be hard pressed to explain the concept of a "normal dissociation," just as it would be difficult to explain the existence of normal splitting or normal projective mechanism outside of a developmental context.

THE NEGATIVE THERAPEUTIC REACTION

The negative therapeutic reaction (NTR) has been a well-known and frequently written about clinical phenomenon since the writings of Sigmund Freud. In a paper published in 1936, "The Problem of the Negative Therapeutic Reaction," Karen Horney described the different clinical types of NTR, and forty years later Asch did the same in a paper entitled "Varieties of Negative Therapeutic Reaction and Problems of Technique" (1976). Most authors agree that these negative therapeutic reactions are defined by patients' unusual response and reactions to the analyst's so-called correct interpretation, which in a cooperative patient will be conducive to insight and improvement in behavior, or lead to an opening of other issues to allow further psychoanalytic exploration. The patient who develops this type of negative reaction to the analyst's interventions sometimes perceives the analyst's "correct interpretation" as a stimulus to compete. The patient may resent perceiving the analyst as able to see something that the patient failed to see or as superior and more articulate than the patient. As Horney pointed out, this type of patient is driven by a need to be perfect and to be admired, and is extremely sensitive to any kind of perceived criticism on the part of the analyst; sometimes the analyst's interpretations are perceived as a criticism of the patient's own grandiosity. Horney points out that the interpretation does not necessarily need to be correct but only perceived by the patient as "brilliant or skillful." At other times an intervention is seen as an accusation, as if the patient is experiencing an unconscious sense of guilt and perceives the analytic process as a trial and the analyst as a judge.

At times, patients have been reported to experience transient remission of symptoms or recovery, only to be followed by despair and discouragement and a wish to terminate the analysis, like the patients identified by Freud as being "wrecked by success." Very frequently underlying this problem is the fear that by being successful, something terrible will happen to their integrity, such as the fear of physical deformity or any other equivalent of castration. So they feel a need to self-defeat and to sabotage any kind of gains they could make in treatment.

The victims of sexual and/or physical abuse are not exempt from the potential development of this complication. We will discuss here the patient's contribution to NTR, and elsewhere we will explore the therapist's contribution to this clinical problem.

Patient's Contribution to NTR

In his paper "Varieties of Negative Therapeutic Reaction and Problems of Technique" Asch (1976) describes the three different types of ego and superego pathology that he considers determinants for the negative therapeutic reaction. He also uses the Freudian concept of unconscious guilt and expands it to a preoedipal determinant of guilt. Asch talks about the pathology of the ego ideal, which he compares with masochism, and also identifies a type of NTR he views as a defense against a regressive, symbiotic fusion. Regarding the ego ideal pathology, Asch maintains that there is a relationship on the part of the patient with a powerful internalized object in which the aim is masochistic suffering. In other words, suffering and punishment is what gratifies the patient, and any interpretation conducive to removing obstacles to this masochistic pleasure will be resisted.

This may be a frequent finding in work with victims of childhood trauma. It is quite common to find structural deficit and superego rigidity as the results of the dysfunctional object relationship. The negative therapeutic reaction ought to be differentiated from the common resistance seen in the analytic process. The major difference is that the patient who develops NTR feels a strong need to fail. Contrary to the typical resistance to change, the need to fail is differentiated from a negative transference in the sense that the transference is the repetition of a childhood event and a negative therapeutic reaction is connected with a specific reaction in the here and now to the therapist's interpretation. Asch formulates his understanding of NTR taking into account an object relations framework and including the pathology of ego ideal development. Whatever the case may be in working with trauma survivors, it is a complication that must be kept in mind.

OTHER COMPLICATIONS

Any severe alteration of the patient's level of psychological functioning outside the therapy sessions should be looked at as a complication of treatment. In addition to the already mentioned specific descriptive syndromes and disorders, we should include any type of severe regression, any psychotic disorder with or without depressive components such as paranoid episodes, delusional disorders, or brief psychotic reactions, as seen frequently in patients with a borderline character presentation when facing acute stressful situations.

Any of these complications will test the clinician to the limit and he or she must be prepared to use whatever clinical resources are necessary to assist the patient out of the crisis.

10

Special Clinical Issues
for the Therapist

THE THERAPIST SURVIVOR – ANONYMITY
VERSUS TRANSPARENCY

A therapist who has been the victim of childhood abuse will be in
a unique situation when treating patients with abuse or trauma
similar to the type the therapist has suffered. On the surface one
can easily comprehend the positive and the negative effects on the
therapeutic process.

The first question is whether the therapist has thoroughly
worked through the trauma. Some individuals are attracted to the
mental health profession because of an unconscious need to understand their own conflicts; at times they try to solve their psychological difficulties in a vicarious manner through their patients. The
therapist may have different degrees of awareness about the issue.
Without receiving proper treatment, the therapist is likely to find
him- or herself under the influence of a variety of internal psychological reactions as the patient discloses details of the abuse, as the
therapeutic process unfolds with all its delicate, elusive dynamism.
It is of paramount importance that if the therapist has a history of

abuse or trauma as a child, adequate treatment should be undertaken prior to any attempt at helping patients with similar problems.

Even after successfully working through their own conflicts, therapists working with traumatized adults should make sure they get appropriate supervision to minimize the possibilities of stalemates, negative therapeutic reactions, negative countertransference reactions, "blind spots," or any adverse or antitherapeutic factors contributing to a lack of progress or premature termination by the patient.

Disclosure by therapists of their own emotional, physical, or sexual abuse to their patients is not appropriate, to say the least; it is not conducive to any therapeutic goal (except perhaps for the therapist) and it may amount to a reversal of roles. It can be argued that disclosing to a patient the therapist's own conflict would create a feeling on the part of the patient that he or she is being easily understood and helps develop an atmosphere of trust. That is hardly the case. Disclosure cannot be confused with the expression of empathy, which is a totally different concept and is not at all related to telling the patient one has had the same traumatic experience. In fact, burdening the patient with the therapist's own traumatic history may be the equivalent of an empathy failure, and may constitute a re-violation and exploitative re-abuse. It is counterproductive and antitherapeutic for the therapist-survivor to disclose such material to the patient.

The transparency of the therapist at times becomes an issue in the therapeutic situation, whether one is working with trauma victims or not. It is even more important for the therapist to maintain anonymity in his or her personal life when working with patients in more expressive-exploratory therapies or psychoanalysis. As mentioned before, there are patients who present a combination of problems, such as a history of trauma embedded in a neurotic disorder, that requires a combination of technical approaches. Breaking the therapist's anonymity and becoming totally transparent to patients deprives them of the therapeutic "mirror" they need to see their real selves and work through their mixed traumatic-neurotic problems.

Socialization with patients not only amounts to a break in the therapeutic contract but to an abandonment of the therapist's responsibility toward the patient; also it could well be experienced by the patient as a revictimization, a repetition by the therapist of the deprivation and abandonment the patient suffered as a child. Socialization will never be conducive to any healing outcome, and the potential for damage to the patient is enormous.

THERAPIST–PATIENT GENDER ISSUE

There has always been much diversity of clinical opinion about what constitutes the best therapeutic gender match. At times, the issue has been divided into what type of disorder is best treated by a male or a female therapist, as if the therapist's gender is the most important healing factor of the therapy. Other issues, such as the quality of the relationship with parents, and whether the conflict was with the father or the mother, have fueled the debate. Sometimes, patients play an important role in perpetuating the myth of an ideal patient–therapist gender match by thinking they can only work with a therapist of their same sex. These notions cause misunderstanding, confusion, and at times clinical stalemates. The outcome of a therapeutic process cannot be predicted on the basis of a patient–therapist gender combination. The factors that intervene in the development of a good therapeutic process are so diverse and unpredictable that the gender role issue becomes a secondary issue, at best, and should not be considered a primary factor at all.

THERAPIST GENDER ISSUES

However, for other authors, the gender of the therapist is undeniably an issue in the treatment of adult survivor patients; that does not, however, mean that same-gender psychotherapy is to be assumed mandatory or correct in every case.

Frequently, patients will have their own gender preference in selecting a psychotherapist. That choice will be based on the past and present circumstances of the individual.

A female therapist is more likely to be chosen by most women patients because they feel more comfortable discussing abuse-related experiences with another woman. Also, a female therapist can be seen as an important role model by the female survivor, and the therapeutic relationship that develops can provide an opportunity for the survivor to identify with and feel more positive about her self-image as a woman and about womanhood in general. The patient's preference should be honored as long as it is not the result of resistance or other factors that will interfere with the therapeutic process. Some authors believe that a therapist should not work with an abused patient if that patient was abused by a perpetrator of the same sex as the therapist, especially when treating sexually abused victims.

Others go even further by commenting, as does Briere (1989), "Because of the potential for revictimization, a number of writers suggest that female abuse survivors should be seen only by female therapists. He recommends that women see women in therapy if an effective female therapist is available or . . . if the client requests one" (p. 76).

The real issue is whether the male therapist has overcome society's bias and whether his upbringing has left him with blind spots that will interfere with the therapy. At times it is a difficult task to decide whether a male therapist is competent enough to work with victims of trauma, male or female. Changes not only in our society as a whole but also the clinical training and quality of supervision are necessary to minimize potential revictimization in the therapy of this patient population.

Of course, not all professional helpers are biased toward same-sex matching between adult survivors and clinicians. It can be argued that because many female adult survivors were abused by a male, having a therapeutic alliance with a proficient male psychotherapist can provide benefits to these women including:

An opportunity to see someone model a healthy male role, thereby counteracting any male sex role prejudices they may have developed as a result of their trauma

The experience of a positive relationship with a male, and all the by-products and rewards of that kind of interaction

The previously impossible development of a sense of trust with a male.

Courtois and Sprei (1988) note that though treating a female incest victim who was abused by a male

> is likely to be more difficult for the male therapist, he should not automatically be assumed to be incompetent to do his work. He will, in all likelihood, have to work harder than his female counterpart to understand the victimization and, in addition, will need to monitor countertransference reactions, especially those having to do with sexual arousal. An opposite-sex supervisor should be considered to assist in exploring and catching problematic gender-related counter-transference reactions. [p. 303]

Women therapists, however, are not immune from socialization biases and cultural influences either. There is a danger that female clinicians will over-relate to a female adult survivor, which in turn may reactivate some of their own unresolved childhood conflicts.

As explained by Herman (1981), "the female therapist generally tends to identify with the victim. Her first reaction to the incest history may be a feeling of helplessness and despair. She correctly recognizes the patient's childhood feelings of betrayal and abandonment, but she may find the feelings so overwhelming that she is unable to react calmly" (p. 182).

Decisions regarding the gender of psychotherapists can logically be made only on a case-by-case basis, taking into consideration patients' individual circumstances and preferences, and the quality of the clinicians of both sexes that are available.

GENDER ISSUES AND TRANSFERENCE

According to the definition of the concept of transference (see chapter 5), the patient's perception of the therapist develops outside the reality of whatever the therapist's gender happens to be. That is, the conflicts generated by a faulty relationship with significant male or female figures in the patient's past are what dictate the color or quality of the transference reaction and what may force the distortion of the perception by the patient. The projection of the internal conflicts and the reenactment of such conflicts in the therapeutic situation have nothing to do dynamically or defensively with the gender of the recipient of the conflict (the therapist); a parent–child conflict is relived in the transference regardless of the therapist's gender. The "penis" may become a "breast" in the midst of a transference reaction and vice versa. Gender by itself as a primordial healing factor in a therapeutic relationship may have been exploited for unclear historical reasons, but it may not withstand an objective clinical scrutiny in a regular practice.

GENDER ISSUES AND COUNTERTRANSFERENCE

There are situations of countertransference reactions that could very well complicate the gender controversy, particularly when the therapist shares a history of childhood abuse. In working with sexually or otherwise physically or emotionally abused adult survivors, the therapist may have a preference (whether conscious or unconscious) to work with only female or male patients.

Being aware of the fact that there are patients the therapist feels more comfortable working with (whether it is the patient's gender or the patient's particular type of psychopathology) usually leads to a better outcome. There are therapists who feel they cannot work with psychopathic or antisocial individuals, as there may be others who avoid working with sexually abused persons; that is a matter of individual choice. But what is crucial is to be aware of blind spots, countertransference reactions (in the broad or narrow definition of such reactions), and not to let those interfere with the therapeutic process. This is solely the responsibility of the therapist. Whether the gender of the patient is an issue for the therapist is the therapist's responsibility to decide. At the risk of overgeneralizing, it can be said the victims of childhood abuse are no different than any other patients when the difficulties in their treatment arise from countertransference reactions stemming from the therapist's own unresolved psychological conflicts.

The technical management of a transference–countertransference reaction of a male patient working with a female therapist is no different than if the same patient were working with a therapist of the same sex. Transference and countertransference do not develop out of gender issues but are internal dynamics unrelated to the patient's or therapist's gender. If the patient raises the issue, particularly after the therapy has started, the therapist should view the situation as reflecting the existence of resistance to the treatment, and should handle it as such. If the issue is brought up by the therapist, who feels uncomfortable with the patient's gender, supervision and/or self-analysis of countertransference is the indicated course of action.

MAINTAINING A HEALTHY PSYCHOLOGICAL FUNCTIONING

Whether or not the therapist is a survivor of childhood abuse(s), it is vital that he or she maintain a healthy, good life balance, both emotionally and interpersonally. Factors that may contribute to maintaining a reasonably good level of psychological functioning (and this may apply to anybody doing psychotherapeutic work, regardless of his or her patient's primary psychopathology) are

1. variety of the caseload
2. professional support
3. balance in life style

Most therapists would agree that having a variety of clinical situations will allow for more satisfaction in daily clinical practice and may prevent burnout. Many therapists would attest to the risk, since even working with the highest functioning patients alone may be at times unhealthy, leading to boredom and lack of clinical stimulation.

The same would apply to working with borderline patients alone, or exclusively with trauma patients. Variety in caseload and changes in the therapist's clinical activities, such as making clinical evaluations, presenting case studies, engaging in hospital work or group therapies, and so on will create additional challenges, prevent boredom, and encourage further development of clinical skills. These activities are complemented by other professional endeavors such as educative projects, supervision, and consultation.

The professional support alluded to above is extremely important not only in maintaining a certain degree of clinical skills but in getting feedback from other professionals in supervisory or consultative roles. It is a healthy way to maintain a high level of professional esteem and a good avenue of support for one's professional superego.

The constant interaction and interchange of ideas with other professionals, whether in consultation or supervision, may strengthen and expand therapists' clinical abilities. At times, it may replace personal psychotherapeutic work clinicians may have previously completed and expand their capacity to accurately assess their own countertransference to patients. We take the position that anyone involved in relatively indepth psychological treatment of patients can benefit a great deal from participating in an individual process to gain insight into his or her own psychic functioning before attempting to help others with their problems. We can only go as deep with our patients as we have gone with ourselves.

Therapists should keep in mind that they should not depend on the outcome of their patients' treatment to feed their self-esteem; it is important to keep a good psychological balance away from the therapeutic practice, which may include a variety of commonsense activities, interests, hobbies, community involvement, and intimate relationships. All will combine to maintain a good balance in lifestyle, which will positively impact clinical practice.

THE ABUSED PATIENT AND THE NEGATIVE THERAPEUTIC REACTION

Even though the development of the negative therapeutic reaction (NTR) belongs to the chapter devoted to complications in work with abused patients, we wish to emphasize a particular component of this clinical phenomenon, that is, the possible contribution of the therapist to the emergence of the negative reaction following seemingly appropriate intervention.

As described initially by Freud in *The Ego and the Id* (1923), a patient with a strong sense of guilt who finds satisfaction in illness may refuse to give up the suffering or the need for self-punishment following a correct interpretation by the therapist. Freud thought that oedipal guilt was the root of this clinical stalemate and he compared it to the dynamics of those "wrecked by success."

Most authors agree that the negative therapeutic reaction is mainly characterized by the patient's unusual response to the therapist's technically well-formulated, "correct" interpretation, which in most patients will be conducive to insight and improvement in behavior or lead to an opening of other issues that allow for further therapeutic exploration.

Whether the underlying dynamic of NTR is oedipal guilt, fear of success, need to compete with and/or defeat the therapist, or envy of the therapist for seeing something in the patient that the patient cannot see, other factors contributed by the therapist may trigger or stimulate the response.

Regardless of how well formulated and correct the therapist's interaction may be, the patient may perceive the therapist as not being able to empathize or understand his conflicts. In working with emotionally, sexually, or physically abused individuals, it is critical not only to convey to patients that their stories are believable but to listen with an empathic ear to patients' past traumatic experience without arriving at premature dynamic formulation and conclusion. A therapist's failure to convey that he or she is trying to understand and give meaning to patients' dramatic feelings, symptoms, and accounts of their trauma, will set the stage for the later development of a lack of positive response to the intervention, however correct it may be.

As has been mentioned in previous chapters, patients with a history of physical, emotional, or sexual abuse enter into a therapeutic relationship with a strong mistrust of others, a fear of being revictimized, and a propensity to perceive the therapist as another potential perpetrator. Any of these might be the fuel needed for an initial negative transference reaction. The therapist should not assume that a negative transference will necessarily lead to a negative therapeutic reaction (a different clinical phenomenon). But in the same way that a negative transference is modified by the therapeutic relationship via internalization of a benign, tolerant, understanding new object (the therapist), by the same token, the therapist can help avoid the development of a negative therapeutic reaction by choosing a reasonable and relatively technically correct intervention, taking an empathic position toward the patient, and allowing him- or herself to experience with the patient the pain and hurt of the trauma without prejudice or preconceived ideas. To think that the child-patient somehow provoked, with repressed oedipal wishes, abuse would most likely be received by the patient as another victimization. Even in some rare cases in which a clear dynamic of such kind is identifiable, it should not be dealt with until the trauma itself has been worked through; the remaining conflicts that are detected and dynamically linked to a neurotic nucleus can then be approached with any appropriate technique the clinician deems necessary.

We postulate that the negative therapeutic reaction should also be differentiated from the common resistance seen in a regular therapeutic process. A patient under the effect of an NTR feels a strong need to fail; it is a reaction in the here and now evoked by a "correct" interpretation and perhaps aided by the therapist's empathic failure. Abused patients are extremely sensitive to the therapist's reaction during the sessions. Maintaining an empathic position "allows the clinician to get inside the patient's ego, experience with the patient the early conflict and use that knowledge to understand the patient's pathology and guide his intervention" (Cruz 1990). An empathic therapist should be able to anticipate within reasonable parameters how the adult survivor of childhood abuse (or any other patient in therapy) may react to a given intervention. Empathy in the last instance may be a manifestation of healthy projective identification used therapeutically.

INTERPRETATION AND THE THERAPIST'S COUNTERTRANSFERENCE REACTION

Interpretation in any therapeutic or analytic process does not take place in a vacuum. Most of the time it is the result of a relationship that has developed over months of working with the patient. Most therapists are familiar with the therapeutic use of countertransferential feelings. In other words, being aware of our reaction to the patient's verbalization can guide our intervention in very meaningful ways. The projective identification frequently used by survivors of abuse as a defense against anxiety can elicit antitherapeutic responses on the part of the therapist. These negative responses are provoked either by the therapist's identification with the patient's projection or by the therapist's empathic failure. Such identification can sometimes create a situation that resembles a negative therapeutic reaction. The therapist's response feeds into the patient's negative perception of the therapist, and may confirm the patient's conviction that the therapist failed to understand his or her conflict.

The therapist's failure to use empathy as a way of anticipating NTR and the therapist's countertransference may both (singly or together) elicit a negative reaction from the patient. These factors are among the most important causes of stalemates in treating this patient population.

11

Clinical Case Studies

A PSYCHOANALYTIC CASE STUDY OF A TRAUMA PATIENT

Mrs. Z. was a married female patient in her late twenties who first came for a consultation with complaints of panic anxiety, insomnia, inability to concentrate and perform at work, restlessness, and feelings of failure and worthlessness. She is a college graduate in good standing in the community. Following a few exploratory interventions and an evaluation, it was felt she was a good candidate for psychoanalytic treatment, as will be elaborated in the next paragraphs.

The diagnosis (*DSM-III-R*) included:

Axis I. Generalized anxiety disorder with panic features

Axis II. Personality disorder with depressive and masochistic features

Axis III. No diagnosis

The patient was in very good physical health and was taking no medication except for occasional use of a mild benzodiazepine for her anxiety episodes.

The patient grew up in a middle-class family in the upper Midwest. She remembered having a very strong, authoritarian mother who was mostly in charge of the discipline at home. She had two siblings. It is worth noticing that she had no recollection whatsoever of any sexual abuse in her childhood. The patient was specifically asked that question as part of the initial evaluation process. She did recall frequent negative experiences, particularly in her relationship with her mother, which she would, at times, describe as emotional abuse and neglect.

Initial Phase

The beginning of the analytic process can be characterized as rather ordinary, in which struggles about establishing a working relationship and developing an atmosphere where emotionally charged issues could be openly ventilated were the main issues.

The patient manifested a capacity to think in psychological terms, and she had a high intellectual capacity. She was very motivated for treatment, and her commitment to the process was excellent. She never missed a session except for rescheduled vacation and she was never late; she was formal and punctual to the point of bordering on the obsessive, something that later was dealt with as part of the analytic process.

During the first year of analysis, her memories about the relationship with her mother were omnipresent. The memories were characterized by a perception of her mother as preferring her sister over her, and never being pleased with her achievements; her perception was that she could never meet the high standards of behavior set by her mother. This translated into a chronic feeling of dissatisfaction and frustration that explained her dysthymia. The overall feeling was that she could never be good enough to accomplish her goals. This put enormous pressure on her to be perfect and intensified the false hope that an ideal performance would get her the approval and admiration of which she felt deprived in her childhood.

> PT: I have a fear of men, of being alone with a man. I don't understand it. I had a relationship with a man which can

be described as a "sugar-daddy" relationship; I fell in love. . . .
I'm not sure what kind of love it was. He got sick and died. I
was angry because he never told me he was sick. [Theme of
fear of abandonment and betrayal that very much dominated
the first few months of analysis]

Next day,

> *PT*: I woke up angry and crying. . . . I'm tired of being an
> adult, of working hard, coping with things, of being positive
> and still being unhappy. I was mad at you when I left last
> night. . . . You invalidated me, interrupted me. . . . I felt I was
> not important to you, as if my feelings were ridiculous. I guess
> I saw you as my parent, like whenever my mother was mad at
> me. If I disagreed with her she could attack me and verbally
> abuse me. . . . I feel that here I'm in a corner and I can't get
> out.
> *TH*: Does it bring anything to mind?
> *PT*: Closeness and intimacy; it also reminds me of being
> home listening to my mother's verbal abuse and not being able
> to stop it. . . . I can't stand it [crying]. . . . I can't go through
> that pain again.

She was very self-critical and harsh on herself whenever she
evaluated her performance in school, at work, or interpersonally.
Even when she could reasonably say she had accomplished her set
goals, she would come up with ways of saying how she could have
handled it in a different way or how she could have done better,
thus perpetuating her dysthymia. This reflected a very demanding
ego ideal, the result of the internalization of a highly demanding
negative introject. It should be mentioned that the patient was a
straight A student with a doctoral degree. That negative mother
introject was omnipresent during this first phase of analysis. As the
patient was able to verbalize and evoke these unpleasant memories,

her fears of retaliation and depressive symptoms gradually began to disappear; she realized that she was not going to be punished for verbalizing her feelings. The internalization of the figure of the analyst as a benevolent introject was toning down the rigidity of the superego–ego ideal system. By the end of the first year of analysis, she was experiencing only sporadic depressive and anxiety symptoms. The use of medication had been discontinued.

Transference Manifestation

The patient's transference reactions were very much characterized by the projection of the highly negative introject onto the analyst, which at times, and particularly in the beginning, took very subtle forms and colors. At times, she conveyed a feeling that she had to make sure that whatever she said during the sessions had to be handled in a way that would not generate a negative reaction from the analyst. Many of the interventions during this initial phase of treatment were formulated to address these particular disguised transference reactions. As the therapeutic alliance grew stronger and she was able to rid herself of the negative feelings about her controlling mother and her passive father, the transference took a more eroticized form.

Middle Phase

This phase was characterized by a shift in her interaction with the analyst to a more sexually stylized manifestation of the transference.

> *PT:* I'm embarrassed about what I want to talk about today; I'm ashamed. . . . I'm horrible. . . . On the weekend I found that my sexual thoughts are coming out frequently and they're getting attached to different people. I'm thinking about jealousy.

TH: What else comes to mind if you let your sexual fantasies come out?

PT: I feel closer to you. . . . Maybe I have sexual feelings toward you. . . . I'm afraid my feelings will ruin our relationship. . . . What's wrong with me? I feel out of control. . . . The more I reveal myself the more vulnerable I feel . . . I fear I may be used by you.

Several weeks later:

PT: I've had a lot of fear. . . . I went to the dentist and I was afraid of being raped. . . . I'm uncomfortable about men, about physical closeness. . . . I've been preoccupied lately about sexual abuse. [Patient went on to recall for the first time some details of her sexual abuse and exploitation by a doctor]

It was during this phase that patient was able to recapture memories about the sexual violation and abuse she experienced growing up that had escaped the evaluation/diagnostic process. She was subjected to sexual exploitation and different kinds of sexual abuse under threat of punishment and intimidation, particularly during her early adolescent period. These experiences clearly had been repressed, as she had no recollection of them until she started to experience erotic fantasies toward the analyst. The color of the transference at that time was a vehicle that facilitated the recovery of her repressed memories. It is our belief that the trauma of the sexual exploitation and abuse was embedded into her neurotic nucleus.

PT: [Brings a dream in which she is with her sister and sister's husband]. Only that he was my previous husband . . . my sister put her hands around my neck as if strangling me. . . . I felt my father licking my fingers. . . . I'm confused because I have sexual feelings toward you; I don't know if you represent my father. . . . I'm afraid of my feelings; I feel I'm bad.

TH: What's wrong about having sexual feelings?

PT: I grew up thinking that it was wrong.

TH: In the dream there is a fluidity of boundaries—

PT: I feel my boundaries were encroached upon. . . . Maybe I don't know my own boundaries. When talking about sexual fantasies, I'm afraid the boundaries are being broken. . . . I was exposed as a child to a lack of boundaries in my immediate family.

TH: What can you expect from me, having had that experience?

PT: That's true. . . . [Silence] Sexual feelings have affected my relationship with men; I'm afraid they destroy relationships.

TH: I wonder how that affected your relationship with your parents?

PT: I feel responsible for what happened at home between my parents; I can't show my sexuality around my parents.

At this junction a technical decision had to be made about whether to view the manifestation of the erotic transference reaction as directly connected with the sexual trauma or whether it had to be dealt with as a developmental issue connected with childhood repressed fantasies associated to oedipal conflicts. Both the trauma of the sexual abuse and the oedipal conflicts appeared to be mixed, embedded, and perhaps reinforcing each other. It was the analyst's technical position to deal with the trauma first, find a resolution to it, and understand all of its ramifications as they impacted the patient's life, leaving all the other elements of the oedipally derived neurotic components for later exploration and analysis. This is an extremely important technical issue in the treatment of many patients, even when they report a history of sexual or physical trauma during the evaluative-diagnostic process. This clinical situation (the combination of repressed sexual abuse and oedipally derived conflicts) can confuse the clinical picture to such a degree that it becomes a source of stalemate. The analyst or therapist may formulate an intervention that seems technically correct (from the point of view of the oedipally derived conflicts) but which leaves the other component (the traumatic event) out of the intervention if not previously worked through. These are cases in which the pseudoneurotic and pseudosexualization of the transference is only a decoy hiding a traumatic event; the reverse could also be true. At any rate, there is a risk that the intervention may be incomplete or inaccurate and may not be well received by the patient, possibly resulting in a negative therapeutic reaction.

It is worth mentioning that once this patient was able to recall one of the events in which she was sexually abused, other memories were uncovered of other repressed abusive episodes. It was not until these traumatic memories were dealt with, clarified, worked through, and given priority that the patient was able to discern in the transference her oedipally derived conflicts.

This vignette illustrates how the beginning of the resolution of the eroticized transference aided in the resolution of the trauma, since both the neurotic nucleus and the impact of the trauma were embedded.

> PT: The feelings I have for you are different than what I had before. . . . I'm lucky I'm doing this work. . . . It's like a new awakening, it's a big step for me. . . . I feel I've gone beyond where I was. I'm stronger and feel better about myself. This has given me a lot of confidence and taken away a lot of

my fears. . . . [Later in the session] Through my relationship with you I've changed. I was feeling unsettled by the sexual feelings and I needed an answer. It's been difficult for me to differentiate sex and love.

TH: The difficulties appear to be around differentiating between parental love and sex.

PT: Yes . . . because I don't know where the boundaries will be broken . . . I am always suspicious of men's intentions and sexual desires.

TH: Why should this man sitting here be the exception?

PT: That's the issue; I feel it could not happen here because I've trusted you and this relationship and this is the first time I've been able to do that. . . . [crying] . . . I feel that if it had happened here I could never trust anybody again.

This middle phase of treatment was also characterized by the beginning of her experiencing anxiety in the face of the progress she was making in analysis and how that progress was translating into an overall improvement in her interpersonal relationships as she continued to take steps to improve her quality of life and anticipate a brighter future. However, anxiety was a constant companion at every step of her progress, meaning a move forward usually intensified her anxiety. Dealing with the pseudosexualization of the transference allowed a resolution of the oedipally derived conflicts, which led to the final phase perhaps better characterized by the exacerbation of her separation anxiety as the analytic process approached its end.

Termination Phase

A Mahlerian-oriented analyst would characterize this phase as being dominated by separation anxiety in the face of progress. This

was experienced during different stages of the patient's development struggles. This feeling was not alien to her, and she had coped
in the past with her anxiety by using a counterphobic mechanism,
such as making impulsive decisions about leaving a situation she
was afraid of leaving in the first place.

An object relations–oriented analyst would view this phase as
the final working-through of the depressive position and anxieties.
The patient was clearly able to see herself in a more integrated way
and realized she had also contributed to the dysfunctional relationship with her parents. Becoming aware of her contribution allowed
her to see herself in a more realistic manner, thus triggering the
depressive anxieties that object relations–oriented analysts or therapists frequently refer to.

Structurally, this final phase was the period during which the
intrapsychic changes were finalized. The ego ideal–superego system
was toned down, bringing about an ability to experience a sense of
gratification, fewer inhibitions, and a resolution of the anxiety
related to the oedipal conflicts.

A self psychology–oriented therapist would think in terms of
transmuting internalization; the patient's need for a self-object was
met, allowing for further growth of the self; this translated into
stronger self-image, self-esteem, and a different way of relating to
herself. An increased capacity to relate to herself in a more functional way translated into better relationships with others. The
working-through of the trauma that created a partial fragmentation
of the self can also be explored from a self-psychological point of
view (as alluded to in a previous chapter).

> PT: [After a brief vacation by the analyst] When I was
> coming here and saw your car I felt a strong need to get
> sexually involved with you, as if I had transformed my feelings
> of abandonment [about analyst's being away] into sexual
> feelings.

TH: [Asks patient to elaborate on her feelings of abandonment]

PT: I felt a sense of panic . . . wondered how I was going to feel as the termination of analysis get closer. . . . I thought to myself, my progress is what increased my feelings of abandonment.

TH: Did your feelings of abandonment precede the sexual ones?

PT: I'm not sure. . . . You were the object of both, the abandonment and sexual feelings. . . . I've seen a change in my attitude and needs for a relationship with a man. . . . I don't feel a need to engage in sex to cope with feelings of deprivation and emptiness. I didn't feel depressed; I didn't feel there was something wrong with me for having those feelings; I know now where they came from. . . . I guess my feelings of abandonment also are connected with the fact that I've become more independent. [Patient was in the process of developing her own business]

The important, crucial therapeutic elements involved here are the analyst's awareness of which theoretical frame or orientation would be more beneficial to the patient at a given point in treatment rather than boxing the patient in a frame that would better fit the analyst's needs.

The clinician should adjust to the vicissitudes of the treatment process and react accordingly, always keeping in mind what is taking place in the intersubjective field.

The patient's depressive anxieties (regardless of the theoretical understanding of the clinician), whether connected with separation, empathic failure, fear of abandonment, or oedipally derived fear of castration, must be worked through, optimally using a flexible approach within the psychodynamic field. The resolution of all of the above vicissitudes yielded to an increased sense of autonomy and a dramatic improvement in the patient's quality of life characterized this final analytic phase.

Several weeks before termination:

> *PT:* It's hard to believe things are going so well for me. . . . I'm a lot more independent and happier now. [silence]
>
> *TH:* What's on your mind?
>
> *PT:* Thinking about how well things are working out for the last several months. . . . Before when I experienced success I was always anxious as if there was never enough. . . . I'm no longer in competition with myself! Now I can enjoy what I've accomplished without saying "It's not good enough." . . . When something doesn't work out now I tell myself, "It's not the end of the world"; that in itself helps me do better. . . . I am not competing with myself!

As the treatment drew to an end she showed an increased capacity to separate from the analytic situation with a gradual lessening of her anxieties. She continued to make great progress in her life, both interpersonally, at work, and in coping with emotionally charged problems.

Summary

This case illustrates several important points, including the fact that the failure to detect trauma of any kind during the evaluation process does not rule out the possibility that the patient has been traumatized; trauma identified during exploratory therapy requires a set of interventions different from those appropriate for a patient whose difficulties are mostly due to an internalized conflict manifesting itself as a discrete neurotic or personality disorder.

Another point illustrated by this situation is how trauma and neurotic conflict can disguise each other, confusing both the technical and etiological pictures.

Finally, this case illustrates that the clinician should be prepared to use whatever theoretical frame best fits the patient's problems. Rigidity, orthodoxy, and inflexibility will handicap the clinician.

THE CASE OF MRS. O.

Mrs. O. was a patient in her early thirties; she was a Catholic woman of Italian extraction who had been married for two years prior to her initial psychiatric evaluation. The patient stated that she wanted no children owing to her own abusive childhood and added, "I don't want to mistreat my children the same way I was mistreated." She was referred by her family physician because her anger was getting out of control, leading to aggressive acts, verbal and physical, against her husband. She stated that the reason for seeking psychotherapy was her desire to eliminate her "irrational" behavior and to exercise control over her anger. She is a college graduate with an outstanding student record, who was then enjoying a highly paid job as an executive.

From the beginning it was clear that she had markedly disturbed schemas manifested by a lack of self-trust, decreased self-confidence, and a strong tendency to blame herself for all her problems. At times, she made statements such as "I am bad," "I am helpless," or "I am to blame." Her self-esteem was obviously low.

She would occasionally devalue herself and had a distorted self-concept, self-image, and body-image; she felt sometimes helpless and powerless, and had an impaired sense of autonomy. It was clear from the start that she was suffering clinically from a combination of generalized anxiety generated by her internal conflict and chronic dysthymia with affective constriction.

Her character structure appeared to be organized at an intermediate level with a combination of both primitive and higher level defenses. Coping mechanisms were centered around idealization versus devaluation and primitive denial; in other situations she would utilize avoidance, repression, less primitive denial, and displacement.

The symptomatology could be grouped as part of a posttraumatic stress disorder, delayed type; her chronic anxiety and irritability translated into recurrent dreams, exaggerated startle responses, intrusive flashbacks, and occasional sleepwalking. Her behavior was at times similar to that seen in compulsive patients, and she suffered from many somatic complaints. She also exhibited fear of closeness and an inability to enjoy her intimate interpersonal interactions.

Right from the start of the evaluation period she expressed herself in a way that led the clinician to believe she was under a great deal of stress. She would anticipate how difficult it would be for her to make any changes in her life. She also found her marriage to be a troublesome situation to adjust to. What precipitated her seeking help was an incident around her wedding anniversary, when she received what she qualified as a "terrible gift" from her husband; she became argumentative and physically violent toward him. She stated, "I became a volcano, fuming for three hours."

Despite the fact that she was so angry at her husband, she also stated that her husband was a "good, Christian, very decent human being." The clinician speculated that she had the potential to be objective in her perception of others—to be able to see both sides of the coin—a developmental milestone (object constancy), something the therapist hoped could be capitalized on in the therapeutic process.

The patient's perception of her husband, whenever she portrayed him in good light, translated into a devaluation of herself and vice versa. When he was good, she was bad; when he was bad, she was good.

These difficulties with her self and object relationships could be traced back to her childhood. She recalled how her father was verbally abusive and how she tried to calm him down. She said she was "the apple of his eye." She recalled violent incidents, her father chasing her brother with a knife and being physically abusive toward him. She would recall being in the middle of the family physical violence. Mrs. O. was very bitter about her childhood experiences and very much resented being put in the role of taking care of her mother and having to translate for her. She, also found herself in the middle of her parents' marital problems, adding, "I became their marriage counselor."

As a child she recalled having many somatic disorders, such as stomach aches, asthma, and different types of allergies. When she was about 16, her father tried to have sex with her. He exposed himself and masturbated while standing up with the door open. "He approached me and made sexual advances; I said no. From then on I became afraid of the dark and locked my bedroom door." Not only did Mrs. O. have to be a marriage counselor, meet her mother's needs, and protect her brother, but she also had to cope with growing up with a sense of deprivation and abandonment, and not being able to meet her own emotional needs. She had to contain her rage and anger while exercising control, and she developed a false self-identity of being good, a tough veneer, and a habit of relating to others in a counterdependent manner to compensate for her feeling "needy and helpless."

Her difficulties with intimacy and closeness could also be traced back to problems arising from feeling let down by her parents. She was hypersensitive to situations of potential rejection stemming from negative, unresolved painful childhood experiences. Her perfectionistic tendencies compensated for her perceived deficiencies, manifesting clinically in the form of highly demanding ego ideal and superego systems. The internalization of these different experiences and the ultimate identification with her dysfunctional parents translated into her depressive symptomatology and, at times, self-defeating and self-destructive tendencies. The rage toward her parents was then redirected toward their internalized parental images, leading to a variety of clinical symptoms.

Initial Phase

Right from the start Mrs. O. came across as an intelligent and articulate person, petite and well dressed. She was usually on time for her appointments. She displayed passive-aggressiveness, and was frequently very verbal and capable of insight. Early on she tried to seek approval from the therapist and wanted to be liked. She showed impulsive behavior at the beginning of her therapy and appeared to have a low tolerance for frustration, which at times led to her exercising poor judgment in her interpersonal interactions. She showed, however, a good capacity for introspection, she trusted the clinician, and she was very motivated to accept help.

One of the characteristics of this initial phase of treatment was her repeated attempts to induce the clinician to play the role of the passive parent; that was the initial color of the emerging transference. Rather than identifying with the projection, the therapist provided her with an atmosphere of support and safety in which she felt accepted by the therapist's non-judgmental attitude and empathic position. The therapist also provided her with a therapeutic framework of well-defined boundaries and rules, which helped in the initial working relationship.

The positive aspect of the transferential reaction was allowed to grow to sustain the therapeutic matrix; sometimes it took the form of an idealized transference. This safe holding environment allowed Mrs. O. to begin to uncover her tough, aggressive veneer without the danger of fragmentation.

Another aspect of this initial phase of treatment was related to the therapist's effort to reframe and correct Mrs. O.'s disturbed schemata, particularly those related to issues of self-blame and poor self-esteem. As she recalled her father's physical and verbal abuses, she remained numb and detached; at times she would look perplexed and would ask with puzzlement why her father was "doing this" to her and what had she done to deserve the abusive behavior, usually ending up blaming the abuses on her "badness."

Session after session, the therapist reframed her distorted beliefs and explained that there was nothing she had done to deserve the abuse she received from her parents. The transformation of these negative self-schemata translated gradually into a different perception of herself, with a reattribution of her childhood abuse to the real offenders, her parents. This, in turn, translated into a decrease in her sense of guilt and shame.

The therapist combined a psychoanalytically oriented approach (self psychology and object relations) with abuse-focused therapy, and psychoeducational and cognitive/behavioral approaches, to fill in the deficits of the self and allow the patient to uncover deeper layers of conflict.

Every layer of conflict worked through led to a strengthening of the therapeutic alliance and allowed her to progress even deeper in her psychological endeavors. The memories about a loss would bring back psychological material about other painful experiences in her childhood, as the grieving process unfolded. She had difficulty modulating and controlling a surge of anxiety and anger on occasions. The therapist remained more attentive during these periods, and tried to maintain meaningful verbal contacts. Silences were frightening to her and brought back how "silences" at home usually preceded violent episodes by her father.

She was slowly able to recognize that the therapist was taking her very seriously and that she was being treated with respect. Toward the end of the initial phase and the beginning of the middle phase, the therapist began to reframe some of the patient's coping mechanisms as "survival" tools that were no longer working for her and that were causing her interpersonal and intrapsychic difficulties.

As the treatment progressed, she was more successful in neutralizing her self-perceptions of helplessness, badness, and worthlessness; this helped in normalizing her self-image and in self-depathologizing, paving the way for the true self to begin to emerge.

Middle Phase

This working-through phase was characterized by a consolidation and final transformation of Mrs. O.'s distorted self-schema into a more realistic, cognitive appraisal of herself; she showed marked clinical improvement during this phase with an overall improvement in her self-esteem. The presenting symptomatology was diminished, and she was more comfortable in her interpersonal relationships, showing a decrease of her sensitivity to what she perceived at times as rejection or abandonment. There was a lesser degree of shame and guilt, and she felt more comfortable showing her inner feelings.

> PT: I think I'm getting worse. . . .
>
> TH: What makes you think that you're getting worse?
>
> PT: I'm feeling different, kind of down, crummy, blah.
>
> TH: Are you saying that you're feeling new uncomfortable feelings and it's scary?
>
> PT: Yes. I don't remember feeling like this . . . strange before—kinda like I'm a child . . . not knowing what to do, how to do it, or when to do it. I don't like feeling like this.
>
> TH: Are you saying that you're feeling helpless and out of control? You're used to feeling in charge and very responsible and you like that feeling much better.
>
> PT: Yes. I like it much better.
>
> TH: Do you ever remember feeling like this, kind of out of control and afraid . . . when you were a child?
>
> PT: Yes. When my father was all out of control, yelling and screaming, attacking my brother and hitting my mother . . . it was awful and I was so scared. I thought he would kill us. I ran into my room and hid under the bed and wanted to cry, but I didn't because I wasn't allowed to cry. Then I came

out of my room to stop him from hurting my mom and brother.

TH: How come you were not allowed to cry?

PT: My parents said it was silly to cry. Only weak people cry. I wanted to be strong.

TH: They didn't understand that it's okay to cry. It's human to cry. Brave people cry too.

PT: [Eyes watering, but she is holding back the tears]

TH: Do you feel sad now and scared too . . . like you did when you were a child?

PT: Yes. Very sad and scared too.

TH: Do you feel like you want to cry, but you are afraid I'll think you're not strong . . . like your parents?

PT: Yes [sniffing].

TH: It's okay to cry. [Pause] It feels good to cry.

PT: [Crying and crying—sobbing]

TH: Yes . . . You feel sad and it's okay to cry. [pause] You need to cry. So much sadness to let go of.

It was very important for the therapist throughout this middle phase to maintain an empathic position. This was considered a vital and central task for the subsequent unfolding of Mrs. O.'s repressed past traumatic material. By now she would attend the therapy session with a sense of vitality, enthusiasm, wittiness, and a sparkle that signified a new inner joy and a sense of well-being; solid progress had been realized.

As the processes of introjection and identification with the therapist as a new benevolent object went on, she began to exhibit a less primitive and less rigid superego–ego ideal system. Her self-perception became more realistic and she was more self-accepting, which translated into an increase in her self-esteem and self-confidence. Her feelings about her femininity were more positive, and she was less threatened by reconnecting with her natural attractive true self; she did not feel less empowered by it. She was in the process of mastering assertiveness and more efficacy in her social and communication skills. She found no need to use a tough veneer to protect herself vis-à-vis male objects. She was beginning to learn other ways to protect her boundaries without sacrificing intimacy.

The nature of the transference changed during this working-through phase. She found herself involved in a strong alliance with the therapist, which allowed for the unfolding of negative experiences that were frequently projected onto the therapist. This gave the therapist an opportunity to use the transference as a therapeutic tool and as a vehicle for further exploration and insight, to allow for a discharge of previously repressed, aggressively charged memories. The quality of the internalized object relationships became clearer as she was able to project onto the therapist her inner world of objects.

This situation obviously created countertransferential feelings, which were also used as therapeutic tools to formulate appropriate, or complementary comments and interventions to promote further psychological growth.

As is the case with most therapeutic processes, the patient did not show linear progress; it was necessary to go back and to rework previous layers of conflict at times, using repeated interpretation of the same issues.

The working-through of each layer of conflict yielded to memories of other painful losses, creating at times a sense of frustration and fear of failure. This was a particularly arduous time for both patient and therapist. The process of unburdening and discharging affect related to so many losses is illustrated in the following transcript.

> PT: I feel so so horrible today. It's so sad about what happened to me . . . the abuses. I'll never know who I would have been.

TH: Are you saying that you're suffering because you were cheated out of ever knowing who you might have become if you had not been abused?

PT: Oh, yes. It's not fair that all these terrible things happened to me and . . . and . . . [pause] I was just an innocent child. I didn't have a fair chance. Oh, God . . . it's not fair—it's not fair!

TH: Of course, it's not fair. You were just a helpless victim—[pause]—an innocent child.

PT: That's right. . . . I missed many chances and now it's gone. I feel awful about all this. . . . [Pause] Such a heaviness deep, deep inside. I missed out on so many things for nothing.

TH: The pain must feel terrible because you lost many of your opportunities during childhood and you think it was in vain. . . . [Pause] No good came from it.

PT: Yeah-h-h. [Silence]

TH: What did you miss most in your childhood?

PT: I missed not having a chance to be a child. To just play, laugh, to have fun . . . to do silly kid things. Lately I've been trying to do some of those things alone or with my husband, but sometimes I even feel sadder.

TH: Are you saying that you were deprived of the fun and carefreeness of childhood and, at times, that makes you very unhappy now?

PT: Yeah [nodding]. . . . I feel so tired of all this and so sad, too.

TH: It's been a long struggle for you. You're feeling deep grief over the loss of freedom to be the child you still long to be. [Therapist is in touch with and recognizes the profound amounts of psychic pain the patient is now experiencing as a result of grieving too many losses at one time. The therapist tries to titrate them and continues]

TH: How does it sound to you if we first concentrate on the loss of freedom and let's put the rest of these back on the shelf for a while until you feel some relief from working through this one.

PT: Uh-huh, sounds fine, but [pause] I still feel miserable.

TH: I know you still feel awful but it might be better if we dealt with some of these losses . . . one at a time.

PT: But, I do feel a little better from talking to you about this.

TH: It helps to talk about your feelings. We'll continue to work these out.

PT: Good . . . Thanks.

Many sessions were devoted to reliving, reworking, and resolving and integrating formerly repressed, traumatic memories of her childhood abuse, particularly the sexual abuse by her father, which was the most arduous for her, even though it was of the noncontact type at age 16. Mrs. O. had denied up to that point that she felt any self-blame for that particular event; she did show the typical aftereffects of cognitive confusion and distorted schemata of self and others (particularly of men) seen frequently in sexually violated or abused children. Anger connected with this event was blocked from expression resulting in repression, denial, and displacement toward her husband.

PT: I was with my parents over the weekend and things seem okay. My dad was behaving fine and then things became ugly.

TH: What do you mean "things became ugly"?

PT: My father became verbally abusive toward me. He put me down for no reason, called me bad names; I felt small and bad.

TH: It sounds like you thought you did something wrong and felt shamed and devalued because your father verbally attacked you.

PT: I felt awful.

TH: Then what happened?

PT: I became so angry but also helpless. I figured that after all those terrible years and because of everything me and my family have suffered due to him, that he would never talk abusive to me anymore.

TH: So once again you were disappointed in your father's behavior. It sounds like you defend yourself from seeing him the way he really is by suppressing his limitations and holding on to unrealistic expectations of him—like unrealistic hope.

PT: My husband says that, too. . . . He says I just don't want to face the truth about my father.

TH: What do you think about what your husband said?

PT: I get so mad at my husband when he talks about my father like that.

TH: Have you ever thought that perhaps it's sometimes easier and safer for you to get angry at your husband rather than at your dad?

PT: Well . . . not really. [Pause]

TH: Does it seem to fit for you?

PT: I don't know . . . maybe.

TH: Would you think about it?

PT: Yes.

TH: Then, what happened next?

PT: It was so terrible. I felt like an anxiety attack was coming on, and my stomach was so upset. It was like a nightmare.

TH: Was your mom there?

PT: Yes.

TH: What did she do?

PT: Nothing as usual. She just looked helpless and wimpy.

TH: Are you saying that you felt so frightened by your father and abandoned by your mom for not protecting you from him?

PT: [Silence] Yeah.

TH: Does that remind you of any other time in the past when you were outraged because he betrayed you and violated your boundaries?

PT: Yes, I hate him, I hate him, I hate him!

TH: Yes. You hate him for hurting you and causing you a lot of pain and suffering.

PT: [Crying, crying] I don't know what I did to him that was so bad.

TH: It doesn't matter what you did. You didn't deserve to be mistreated and abused. You are not responsible for your father's behavior.

PT: That's right. I'm not.

Session after session during this phase of treatment, the therapist encouraged cognitive reappraisals and helped the patient pace and discharge her repressed affect. As the patient began to enjoy newly found pleasure in her relationships with others, she started to struggle with other developmental and motivational issues. Her progress at times activated a feeling that getting well was equal to a betrayal of her parent. "How can I feel so happy when my mother is such an unhappy person" threatened to undo territory gained. At times, she verbalized a fear of doing well only to have someone take it away from her, as if she would activate a pathological object relations unit dominated by withdrawal of affection and support in the face of her doing well and becoming independent. Sometimes she had a strong sense that by undoing her progress she would recapture the previously withdrawn support and affection. This remained one of her main struggles as she approached the end of the working-through phase.

The therapist continued to use an eclectic psychodynamic approach in combination with cognitive, trauma theory–derived techniques, as well as psychoeducational and behavioral technical interventions. This combination of interventions proved most efficient in treating Mrs. O.

Issues about autonomy—separation–individuation themes— took the front line as trauma-related conflicts began to subside together with the psychosomatic symptomatology.

By this time, Mrs. O. had decided to have a child; this was an event with tremendous symbolic meaning. As she was becoming a new psychological being, she decided to give birth to a child. A clear intrapsychic change had taken place, and it allowed for a more fulfilling life. This characterized the end of the middle phase of her treatment.

Termination Phase

One day toward the end of the second year of therapy, Mrs. O. bounced into the office, her face aglow.

> *TH*: You look elated today. There is a glow about you that I've not seen before. It's very becoming.
>
> *PT*: I am so-o-o thrilled. I wanted you to be one of the very first to know . . . I'm going to have a baby. [Pause] I haven't even told my parents yet.
>
> *TH*: [Happy tears in her eyes and a large smile on her face, knowing that this was the best evidence that Mrs. O. had

overcome her childhood trauma] I'm so happy for you. Tell me all about it.

PT: I'm pregnant and I didn't even think I would become pregnant so fast. We just really started trying. I'm so happy . . . so thrilled. I'm going to nurture this child in all the best ways. I want to give the baby a place of peace—a soothing atmosphere—gentleness—no abuse ever. I don't think I'm going to let my father be alone with the baby. I want a girl so that I can take care of her in the special ways that I've learned and am now caring for myself. I want to give her so much love, warmth and I'll accept her—or him—for who they are.

TH: You want to give her a safe environment, full of new opportunities for love and all that's healthy.

PT: Yes. All the things that I deserved as a child and that all children in the world deserve . . . to be free from harm.

TH: You want to give her good treatment, full of rich potential and you wish all children could grow up without being injured.

Mrs. O. continued to seek psychotherapy on a biweekly basis; she continued to consolidate her gains and dealt with new challenges as well as the old issues. She developed a greater ego capacity, which manifested in better control of her impulses, healthier coping mechanisms, and a better capacity to manage situations of anxiety or stress. She was never on medication during her entire course of treatment. She was more aware of her needs and able to meet them in a healthy way. She became more introspective and less afraid of self-examination. She also became more empathic toward others and capable of altruistic behavior. Her boundaries became clearer. She developed a wide range of feelings while expressing them appropriately, and her affect constriction disappeared; this went together with a better capacity to be alone.

She felt empowered and assertive. Her capacity to trust others and her self-confidence were markedly improved. She developed the capacity to self-soothe and calm herself when feeling distressed, as well as the ability to regulate her self-esteem. She eliminated self-blame for the abuse and trauma and forgave her parents, herself, and others. She verbalized a new capacity to enjoy intimacy without feeling threatened in her own identity. The ego ideal–superego system was toned down, translating into more tolerance of her own and others' limitations.

When individuals are allowed to be free to be their true selves in a safe, trusting, holding environment with respect and without judgment, the opportunities for developing their unique selves are limitless.

References

Ammerman, R. (1991). The role of the child in physical abuse: a reappraisal. *Violence and Victims* 6:87–97.

Armsworth, M. (1989). Therapy of incest survivors: abuse or support? *Child Abuse & Neglect* 13:549–561.

Asch, S. (1976). Varieties of negative therapeutic reaction and problems of technique. *Journal of the American Psychoanalytic Association* 24:383–408.

Basta, S., and Peterson, R. (1990). Perpetrator status and the personality characteristics of molested children. *Child Abuse & Neglect* 14:555–565.

Beres, D. (1956). Ego deviation and the concept of schizophrenia. *Psychoanalytic Study of the Child.* Vols. 1–25 (1945–1970). New York: International Universities Press.

Bibring, E. (1954). Psychoanalysis and the dynamic psychotherapies. *Journal of the American Psychoanalytic Association* 2:745–770.

Biestek, F. (1957). *The Casework Relationship.* Chicago: Loyola University Press.

Braun, B. (1989). The basic model of dissociation. *Dissociation* 1:4–23.

Briere, J. (1989). *Therapy for Adults Molested as Children.* New York: Springer.

—— (1992). *Child Abuse Trauma.* Newbury Park, CA: Sage.

Briere, J., Evans, D., Runtz, M., and Walls, T. (1988). Symptomatology in men who were molested as children: a comparison study. *American Journal of Orthopsychiatry* 58: 457–461.

Briere, J., and Runtz, M. (1988). Multivariate correlates of childhood psychological and physical maltreatment among university women. *Child Abuse & Neglect* 12:331–341.

—— (1990). Differential adult symptomatology associated with three types of child abuse histories. *Child Abuse & Neglect* 14:357–364.

Browne, A., and Finkelhor, D. (1986a). Impact of child sexual abuse: a review of the research. *Psychological Bulletin* 99:66–77.

—— (1986b). Initial and long-term effects: a review of the research. In *A Sourcebook on Child Sexual Abuse*, ed. D. Finkelhor. Beverly Hills, CA: Sage.

Burgess, A. W., and Holstrom, L. C. (1974). Rape trauma syndrome. *American Journal of Psychiatry* 131:981–986.

Claussen, A., and Crittenden, P. (1991). Physical and psychological maltreatment: relations among types of maltreatment. *Child Abuse & Neglect* 15:5–15.

Courtois, C. A. (1988). *Healing the Incest Wound: Adult Survivors in Therapy.* New York: W. W. Norton.

Courtois, C., and Sprei, J. (1988). Retrospective incest therapy for women. In *Handbook on Sexual Abuse of Children*, ed. L. E. Walker, pp. 270–308. New York: Springer.

Courtois, C., and Watts, D. (1982). Counseling adult women who experienced incest in childhood or adolescence. *Personnel and Guidance Journal*, pp. 275–279.

Cruz, F. (1990). Empathic failure and the negative therapeutic reaction. Unpublished paper.

Danieli, Y. (1989). Mourning in survivors and children of survivors of the Nazi holocaust: the role of group and community modalities. In *The Problem of Loss and Mourning: Psychoanalytic Perspectives*, eds. D. Dietrich, and P. Shabad. New York: International Universities Press.

Deffenbacher, J., and Suinn, R. (1987). Generalized anxiety syndrome. In *Anxiety and Stress Disorders*, eds. L. Michelson, and M. Ascher. New York: Guilford.

Elliott, D., and Briere, J. (1992). Sexual abuse trauma among professional women: validating the trauma symptom checklist-40 (TSC-40). *Child Abuse & Neglect* 16:391–397.

Everstine, D., and Everstine, L. (1989). *Trauma in Children and Adolescents: Dynamics and Treatment*. New York: Brunner/Mazel.

Figley, C., ed. (1985). *Trauma and Its Wake*. Vol. 1. *The Study of and Treatment of Post-Traumatic Stress Disorder*. New York: Brunner/Mazel.

—— (1986). *Trauma and Its Wake*. Vol. 2. *Traumatic Stress Theory Research, and Intervention*. New York: Brunner/Mazel.

Finkelhor, D., and Browne, A. (1985). The traumatic impact of sexual abuse: a conceptualization. *American Journal of Orthopsychiatry* 55:530–541.

Flavell, J. (1963). *The Developmental Psychology of Jean Piaget*. Princeton, NJ: Van Nostrand.

Flournoy, P., and Wilson, G. (1991) Assessment of MMPI profiles of male batterers. *Violence and Victims* 7:309–317.

Forward, S., and Buck, C. (1979). *Betrayal of Innocence*. New York: Penguin.

Francis, C., Hughes, H., and Hitz, L. (1992). Physically abusive parents and the 16PF: a preliminary psychological typology. *Child Abuse & Neglect* 16:673–683.

Freud, A. (1936). *The Ego and Its Mechanisms of Defense*. New York: International Universities Press, 1946.

Freud, S. (1900). The interpretation of dreams. *Standard Edition* 4/5:1–626.

—— (1905a). Fragment of an analysis of a case of hysteria. *Standard Edition* 7:3–122.

—— (1905b). Three essays on the theory of sexuality. *Standard Edition* 7:121–245.

—— (1911). Formulations on the two principles of mental functioning. *Standard Edition* 12:213–226.

—— (1920). Beyond the pleasure principle. *Standard Edition* 18:3–64.

—— (1923). The ego and the id. *Standard Edition* 19:3–68.

—— (1926). Inhibition, symptoms and anxiety. *Standard Edition* 20:87–172.

Garbarino, J., Guttmann, E., and Seeley, J. (1986). *The Psychologically Battered Child.* San Francisco, CA: Jossey-Bass.

Garrison, E. (1987). Psychological maltreatment of children. *American Psychologist* 42:157–159.

Gelinas, D. (1983). The persisting negative effects of incest. *Psychiatry* 46:312–332.

—— (1988). Family therapy: characteristic family constellation and basic therapeutic stance. In *Vulnerable Populations*, vol. 1, ed. S. M. Sgroi. Lexington, MA: Lexington Books.

Gelles, R. (1980). Violence in the family: a review of research in the seventies. *Journal of Marriage and the Family* 42:873–885.

Gil, E. (1983). *Outgrowing the Pain: A Book for and about Adults Abused as Children.* Rockville, MD: Launch Press.

—— (1988). *Treatment of Adult Survivors of Childhood Abuse.* Walnut Creek, CA: Launch Press.

Gill, M. (1954). Psychoanalysis and exploratory psychotherapy. *Journal of the American Psychoanalytic Association* 2:771–797.

Goldstein, E. (1984). *Ego Psychology and Social Work Practice.* New York: The Free Press.

Hamilton, N. (1990). *Self and Others: Object Relations Theory in Practice.* Northvale, NJ: Jason Aronson.

Hart, S. N., Germain, R., and Brassard, M. R. (1987). The challenge: to better understand and combat the psychological maltreatment of children and youth. In *Psychological Maltreatment of Children and Youth*, ed. M. R. Brassard, R. Germain, and S. N. Hart, pp. 3–24. New York: Pergamon.

Hartman, N. (1939). *Ego Psychology and the Problem of Adaptation.* New York: International Universities Press.

Haugaard, J., and Reppucci, N. (1988). *The Sexual Abuse of Children.* San Francisco CA: Jossey-Bass.

Herman, J. L. (1981). *Father–Daughter Incest*. Cambridge, MA: Harvard University Press.

_____ (1992). *Trauma and Recovery*. New York: Basic Books.

Herman, J. L., Russell, D. E., and Trocki, K. (1986). Long-term effects of incestuous abuse in childhood. *American Journal of Psychiatry* 143:1293–1296.

Hinsie, L., and Campbell, R. (1974). *Psychiatric Dictionary*, 4th ed. New York: Oxford University Press.

Horner, A. (1991). *Psychoanalytic Object Relations Therapy*. Northvale, NJ: Jason Aronson.

Horney, K. (1936). The problem of the negative therapeutic reaction. *Psychoanalytic Quarterly* 5:29–44.

Husley, T., Sexton, M., and Nash, M. (1992). Perception of family functioning and the occurrence of childhood sexual abuse. *Bulletin of the Menninger Clinic* 56:438–450.

Horowitz, M. (1986). *Stress Response Syndromes*. Northvale, NJ: Jason Aronson.

Jehu, D. (1988). *Beyond Sexual Abuse: Therapy with Women Who Were Childhood Victims*. Chichester, U.K.: Wiley.

Karush, A. (1967). Working through. *Psychoanalytic Quarterly* 36:497–531.

Kelly, L. (1988). *Surviving Sexual Violence*. Minneapolis: University of Minnesota Press.

Kempe, C., Silverman, F. N., Steele, B. F., et al. (1962). The battered-child syndrome. *Journal of the American Medical Association* 181:17–24.

Kernberg, O. (1970). A psychoanalytic classification of character pathology. *Journal of the American Psychoanalytic Association* 18:800–820.

_____ (1976). *Object Relations Theory and Clinical Psychoanalysis*. New York: Jason Aronson.

_____ (1980). *Internal World and External Reality*. New York: Basic Books.

_____ (1984). *Severe Personality Disorder: Psychotherapeutic Strategies*. New Haven: Yale University Press.

Klein, M. (1932). *The Psycho-Analysis of Children*. London: Hogarth.

—— (1940). Mourning and its relation to manic-depressive states. In *Contributions to Psycho-Analysis 1921–1945*. London: Hogarth.

—— (1957a). *Envy and Gratitude*. London: Tavistock.

—— (1957b). On identification. In *New Directions in Psycho-Analysis*, pp. 309–345. New York: Basic Books.

Klein, M., and Tribich, D. (1981). Kernberg's object relations theory: a critical evaluation. *International Journal of Psycho-Analysis* 62:27–43.

Kohut, H. (1971). *The Analysis of the Self*. New York: International Universities Press.

—— (1977). *The Restoration of the Self*. New York: International Universities Press.

Kohut, H., and Wolf, E. S. (1978). The disorders of the self and their treatment: an outline. *International Journal of Psycho-Analysis* 59:413–425.

Kottler, J. (1991). *The Compleat Therapist*. San Francisco, CA: Jossey-Bass.

Laplanche, J., and Pontalis, J. B. (1973). *The Language of Psycho-Analysis*. New York: W. W. Norton.

Leehan, J., and Wilson, L. (1985). *Grown-Up Abused Children*. Springfield, IL: Charles C Thomas.

Lister, E. (1982). Forced silence: a neglected dimension of trauma. *American Journal of Psychiatry* 139:872–875.

Mahler, M. S., Pine, F., and Bergman, A. (1975). *The Psychological Birth of the Human Infant*. New York: Basic Books.

Maltz, W., and Holman, B. (1987). *Incest and Sexuality: A Guide to Understanding and Healing*. Lexington, MA: Lexington Books.

Martin, J., and Elmer, E. (1992). Battered children grow up: a follow-up study of individuals severely maltreated as children. *Child Abuse & Neglect* 16:75–86.

Masterson, J. (1976). *Psychotherapy of the Borderline Adult*. New York: Brunner/Mazel.

McCann, I., and Perlman, L. (1990). *Psychological Trauma and the Adult Survivor: Theory, Therapy and Transformation*. New York: Brunner/Mazel.

Moran, P., and Eckenrode, J. (1992). Protective personality characteristics among adolescent victims of maltreatment. *Child Abuse & Neglect* 16:743–752.

National Center on Child Abuse and Neglect (1988). *National Incidence and Prevalence of Child Abuse and Neglect*. Washington, DC.

_____ (1990). *National Incidence and Prevalence of Child Abuse and Neglect*. Washington, DC.

Okula, S. (1987). Abusive child–parent theory dispelled. Associated Press, September.

Perlman, H. (1979). *Relationship: The Heart of Helping People*. Chicago: University of Chicago Press.

Piaget, J. (1932a). *The Language and Thought of the Child*. New York: Harcourt, Brace & World.

_____ (1932b). *The Moral Judgement of the Child*. New York: Harcourt, Brace & World.

_____ (1952). *The Origin of Intelligence in Children*. New York: International Universities Press.

_____ (1963). *The Child's Conception of the World*. Paterson, NJ: Sittlefield, Adams.

_____ (1967). *Six Psychological Studies*. New York: Vintage.

Price, G. (1990). Non-rational guilt in victims of trauma. *Dissociation* 3:160–164.

Putnam, F. W. (1989). *Diagnosis and Treatment of Multiple Personality Disorder*. New York: Guilford.

Reiker, P. P., and Carmen, E. (1986). The victim-to-patient process: the disconfirmation and transformation of abuse. *American Journal of Orthopsychiatry* 56:360–370.

Rogers, C. (1961). *On Becoming a Person*. Boston: Houghton Mifflin.

Rowe, C., and Mac Isaac, D. (1989). *Empathic Attunement: The "Technique" of Psychoanalytic Self Psychology*. Northvale, NJ: Jason Aronson.

Russell, D. (1984). *Sexual Exploitation: Rape, Child Sexual Abuse, and Workplace Harassment*. Newbury Park, CA: Sage.

Scharff, J. S. (1992). *Projective and Introjective Identification and the Use of the Therapist's Self*. Northvale, NJ: Jason Aronson.

Schellenback, C., Trickett, P., and Susman, E. (1991). A multi-method approach to the assessment of physical abuse. *Violence and Victims* 6:57–71.

Sgroi, S. M. (1988). *Vulnerable Populations.* Vol 1. Lexington, MA: Lexington Books.

_____ (1989). *Vulnerable Populations.* Vol. 2. Lexington, MA: Lexington Books.

Shengold, L. (1989). *Soul Murder.* New Haven: Yale University Press.

Slap, J. (1987). Implications for the structural model of Freud's assumptions about perception. *Journal of the American Psychoanalytic Association* 35:629–646.

Steele, B. (1986). Notes on the lasting effects of early child abuse throughout the life cycle. *Child Abuse & Neglect* 10:283–291.

Sterba, R. (1951). A case of brief psychotherapy by Sigmund Freud. *Psychoanalytic Review* 35:70–75.

Summit, R. (1983). The child sexual abuse accommodation syndrome. *Child Abuse & Neglect* 7:177–193.

Ticho, E. (1970). Differences between psychoanalysis and psychotherapy. *Bulletin of the Menninger Clinic* 34:128–139.

Tolman, R., and Bennett, L. (1990). A review of quantitative research on men who batter. *Journal of Interpersonal Violence* 5:87–112.

Ulman, R., and Brothers, D. (1988). *The Shattered Self.* Washington, DC: American Psychiatric Press.

Vissing, Y., and Straus, M. (1991). Verbal aggression by parents and psychological problems of children. *Child Abuse & Neglect* 15:223–236.

Walker, L. (1979). *The Battered Woman.* New York: Harper & Row.

_____ (1988). *Handbook on Sexual Abuse of Children.* New York: Springer.

Walker, C., Bonner, B., and Kaufman, K. (1988). *The Physically and Sexually Abused Child.* New York: Pergamon.

Weikel, D., and Krupinski, E. (1986). *Death from Child Abuse . . . And No One Heard.* Winter Park, FL: Currier-Davis.

Wilson, J. (1989). *Trauma, Transformation and Healing*. New York: Brunner/Mazel.

Winnicott, D. W. (1965). *The Maturational Processes and the Facilitating Environment*. New York: International Universities Press.

Wolff, P. (1960). The developmental psychologies of Jean Piaget and psychoanalysis. *Psychological Issues*, Vol. 2, no. 2, monograph 5.

Index